2nd Workshop on Computational Models of Reference, Anaphora and Coreference (CRAC 2019)

Minneapolis, Minnesota, USA
7 June 2019

ISBN: 978-1-5108-8782-4

Printed from e-media with permission by:

Curran Associates, Inc.
57 Morehouse Lane
Red Hook, NY 12571

Some format issues inherent in the e-media version may also appear in this print version.

Printed by Curran Associates, Inc. (2019)

For permission requests, please contact the Association for Computational Linguistics at the address below.

Association for Computational Linguistics
209 N. Eighth Street
Stroudsburg, Pennsylvania 18360

Phone: 1-570-476-8006
Fax: 1-570-476-0860

acl@aclweb.org

Additional copies of this publication are available from:

Curran Associates, Inc.
57 Morehouse Lane
Red Hook, NY 12571 USA
Phone: 845-758-0400
Fax: 845-758-2633
Email: curran@proceedings.com
Web: www.proceedings.com

NAACL HLT 2019

Second Workshop on Computational Models of Reference, Anaphora and Coreference

Proceedings of the Workshop

June 7, 2019
Minneapolis, USA

Introduction

This is the second edition of the Workshop on Computational Models of Reference, Anaphora and Coreference (CRAC), which was first held in New Orleans last year in conjunction with NAACL HLT 2018. CRAC and its predecessor, the Coreference Resolution Beyond OntoNotes (CORBON) workshop series that started in 2016, have arguably become the primary forum for coreference researchers to present their latest results since the demise of the Discourse Anaphora and Anaphor Resolution Colloquium series in 2011. While CORBON focuses on under-investigated coreference phenomena, CRAC has a broader scope, covering all cases of computational modeling of reference, anaphora, and coreference.

The workshop received 10 submissions: half of them were from Europe, two were from the U.S., and the remaining three were from India. We are pleased to see that the submissions covered not only a variety of less-studied languages in the coreference community (e.g., Basque, French, German, Malayalam or Tamil) but also many under-investigated topics in coreference resolution (e.g., feature representation, coreference for low-resource languages, coreference in specialized domains, and evaluation of coreference resolvers). While it is perhaps not surprising to receive submissions focusing on the design and use of neural models for coreference resolution given the recent popularity of deep learning for natural language processing, it is interesting to see that the most popular topic among the submitted papers is cross-lingual coreference resolution. In fact, one of the workshop sessions will be devoted entirely to this topic.

As in previous years, each submission was rigorously reviewed by three to five programme committee members. We would like to thank the 18 programme committee members for their hard work. Based on their recommendations, we initially accepted four papers and conditionally accepted two papers. Both conditionally accepted papers were eventually accepted to the workshop after we made sure that the authors adequately addressed the reviewers' comments in the final camera-ready version. All of the accepted papers will be presented orally.

We are grateful to Amir Zeldes for accepting our invitation to be this year's invited speaker. Amir will give a talk on coreference, discourse structure and coherence.

Finally, we would like to thank the workshop participants for joining in. We look forward to an exciting workshop in Minneapolis.

— Maciej Ogrodniczuk, Sameer Pradhan, Yulia Grishina, and Vincent Ng

Organizing Committee and Proceedings Editors:

Maciej Ogrodniczuk, Institute of Computer Science, Polish Academy of Sciences
Sameer Pradhan, cemantix.org and Vassar College
Yulia Grishina, Amazon
Vincent Ng, University of Texas at Dallas

Programme Committee:

Antonio Branco, University of Lisbon
Stephanie Dipper, University of Bochum
Yulia Grishina, Amazon
Veronique Hoste, Ghent University
Ryu Iida, National Institute of Information and Communications Technology (NICT)
Sandra Kübler, Indiana University
Sobha Lalitha Devi, AU-KBC Research Center, Anna University of Chennai
Emmanuel Lassalle, Machina Capital, Paris
Katja Markert, Heidelberg University
Pavankumar Reddy Muddireddy, Google
Costanza Navaretta, University of Copenhagen
Anna Nedoluzhko, Charles University in Prague
Michal Novak, Charles University in Prague
Constantin Orasan, University of Wolverhampton
Massimo Poesio, Queen Mary University of London
Marta Recasens, Google
Yannick Versley, IBM
Heike Zinsmeister, University of Hamburg

Invited Speaker:

Amir Zeldes, Georgetown University

Table of Contents

Workshop Program: June 7, 2019

09:00–10:30 Session 1: Welcome and Invited Talk

09:00–09:15 *Introduction*
Vincent Ng and Sameer Pradhan

09:15–10:30 Invited talk: *Coreference and Coherence Revisited*
Amir Zeldes

10:30–11:00 Mid-Morning Break

11:00–12:30 Session 2

11:00–11:30 *Evaluation of Named Entity Coreference*
Oshin Agarwal, Sanjay Subramanian, Ani Nenkova and Dan Roth

11:30–12:00 *Neural Coreference Resolution with Limited Lexical Context and Explicit Mention Detection for Oral French*
Loïc Grobol

12:00–12:30 *Entity Decisions in Neural Language Modelling: Approaches and Problems*
Jenny Kunz and Christian Hardmeier

12:30–14:00 Lunch Break

14:00–15:30 Session 3

14:00–14:30 *Cross-lingual NIL Entity Clustering for Low-resource Languages*
Kevin Blissett and Heng Ji

14:30–15:00 *Cross-lingual Incongruences in the Annotation of Coreference*
Ekaterina Lapshinova-Koltunski, Sharid Loáiciga, Christian Hardmeier and Pauline Krielke

15:00–15:30 *Deep Cross-Lingual Coreference Resolution for Less-Resourced Languages: The Case of Basque*
Gorka Urbizu, Ander Soraluze and Olatz Arregi

15:30–16:00 Mid-Afternoon Break

16:00–17:00 Session 4

16:00–17:00 *Informal Discussion and Closing Remarks*
Sameer Pradhan

Evaluation of Named Entity Coreference

Oshin Agarwal *
University of Pennsylvania
oagarwal@seas.upenn.edu

Sanjay Subramanian *
University of Pennsylvania
subs@seas.upenn.edu

Ani Nenkova
University of Pennsylvania
nenkova@seas.upenn.edu

Dan Roth
University of Pennsylvania
danroth@seas.upenn.edu

Abstract

In many NLP applications like search and information extraction for named entities, it is necessary to find all the mentions of a named entity, some of which appear as pronouns (she, his, etc.) or nominals (the professor, the German chancellor, etc.). It is therefore important that coreference resolution systems are able to link these different types of mentions to the correct entity name. We evaluate state-of-the-art coreference resolution systems for the task of resolving all mentions to named entities. Our analysis reveals that standard coreference metrics do not reflect adequately the requirements in this task: they do not penalize systems for not identifying any mentions by name to an entity and they reward systems even if systems find correctly mentions to the same entity but fail to link these to a proper name (she–the student–no name). We introduce new metrics for evaluating named entity coreference that address these discrepancies and show that for the comparisons of competitive systems, standard coreference evaluations could give misleading results for this task. We are, however, able to confirm that the state-of-the art system according to traditional evaluations also performs vastly better than other systems on the named entity coreference task.

1 Introduction

Coreference resolution is the task of identifying all expressions in text that refer to the same entity. In this paper we set out to provide an in-depth analysis of the task specifically for named entities: finding all references—either by name, pronoun or nominal—to a named entity in the text.

Many language technology tasks focus on entities and our work is oriented towards practical uses of the results of coreference resolution in downstream tasks. Named entities are often targets for information extraction (Ji and Grishman, 2011), biography summarization (Zhou et al., 2004) and knowledge base completion tasks (West et al., 2014). More relevant information can be extracted for these tasks if we also know which pronouns and nominals refer to the entity. Similarly, creation of proper noun ontologies (Mann, 2002) can use patterns other than (proper noun–common noun) if other references to the entity are known.

Recent work (Webster et al., 2018) has shown that standard coreference datasets are biased and high performance on these need not mean high performance in downstream tasks. We argue that the standard coreference metrics are not suitable either from the perspective of downstream applications. Since applications require information about entities and entities are usually identified by their names, the evaluation metrics should focus on the resolution of mentions to the correct name. If all the pronouns referring to an entity are resolved correctly to each other but are not linked to any name or are linked to a wrong name, the results would not be useful for downstream tasks. Standard coreference metrics do not incorporate these aspects and hence give high performance for results unsuitable for further use. We also show that the existing metrics are not sensitive to finding any mention to an entity at all. They give higher performance for systems that do not find a large number of entities but do good coreference resolution on the subset of entities they find.

This problem of coreference chains without any named mentions being unsuitable has previously been discussed in (Chen and Ng, 2013). The authors argued that a name is more informative than a nominal, which is more informative than a pronoun so they assign different weights to co-reference links (mention-antecedent pairs) in a chain depending on the type of mentions the link contains. They assign a higher weight to

*equal contribution

Proceedings of the 2nd Workshop on Computational Models of Reference, Anaphora and Coreference (CRAC 2019), pages 1–7,
Minneapolis, USA, June 7, 2019.

a link having a name than one that doesn't and also higher weight to a link having a nominal than a link that contains just pronouns. Similarly, (Martschat and Strube, 2014) perform an error analysis for co-reference by choosing an antecedent that is a name or a nominal in this order because they are more informative than a pronoun. However, we argue that we should view the coreference chains as a whole instead of individual links when evaluating systems for downstream application. If a chain contains even one named mention, it should be sufficient for using it in applications and we need not consider the mention type in each link within the chain.

We introduce metrics focused on Named Entity Coreference (NEC) which separate the identification of entities and resolution of different mention types, thus tackling the above issue and transparently tracking areas of system improvement.

2 Coreference Evaluation

Shared tasks on coreference (at CoNLL-2011 and 2012 (Pradhan et al., 2014)) use the average of three F1 scores as their official evaluation: MUC (Vilain et al., 1995), B^3 (Bagga and Baldwin, 1998) and CEAFE (Luo, 2005). Prior work (Moosavi and Strube, 2016) discussed shortcoming of these metrics and introduced the improved link entity aware (LEA) score. Below we describe each score in the context of downstream tasks. Let K be the set of key (gold) clusters, and let R be the set of response clusters.

MUC The recall for an entity is the minimum number of links that would have to be added in the predicted clusters containing any mention of this entity, to make them connected and part of the same cluster. Precision is computed by reversing the role of gold and predicted clusters.

$$\text{Recall} = \frac{\sum_{k_i \in K} |k_i| - |p(k_i)|}{\sum_{k_i \in K}(|k_i| - 1)}$$

where $p(k_i)$ is the partition of k_i generated by intersecting k_i with the response entities.

Gold: {JohnDoe, he_1, he_2, he_3} {RichardRoe, he_4, he_5}
Solution 1: {JohnDoe, he_1, he_2} {RichardRoe, he_4}
Solution 2: $\{he_1, he_2, he_3\}\{he_4, he_5\}$

Table 1: Hypothetical Solution 2 has no practical value.

B-cubed B^3 works on the mention level. It iterates over all gold-standard mentions of an entity, averaging the recall of its gold cluster in its predicted cluster. It computes precision by reversing the role of gold and predicted clusters.

$$\text{Recall} = \frac{\sum_{k_i \in K} \sum_{r_j \in R} \frac{|k_i \cap r_j|^2}{|k_i|}}{\sum_{k_i \in K} |k_i|}$$

CEAF CEAF first maps each gold cluster to a predicted cluster. It then computes recall as the number of similar mentions shared by the gold and predicted clusters divided by the number of mentions in the gold cluster. Precision is equal to the number of similar mentions shared by the gold and predicted, divided by the number of mentions in the predicted cluster. Numbers are reported either per mention (CEAFm), or per entity (CEAFe).

$$\text{Recall} = \frac{\sum_{k_i \in K^*} \phi(k_i, g^*(k_i))}{\sum_{k_i \in K} \phi(k_i, k_i)}$$

where K^* is the set of key entities in the optimal one-to-one mapping and $\phi(\cdot,\cdot)$ is a similarity measure for a pair of entities. In CEAFm, $\phi(k_i, r_j) = |k_i \cap r_j|$, and in CEAFe, $\phi(k_i, r_j) = \frac{2|k_i \cap r_j|}{|k_i| + |r_j|}$.

LEA Recall is computed as the fraction of correctly resolved links between mentions. Results for each entity are weighted by its number of mentions, so that resolving correctly an entity with more mentions contributes more to the overall score. Precision is computed by reversing the role of gold and predicted clusters.

$$\text{Recall} = \frac{\sum_{k_i \in K} \left[|k_i| \times \sum_{r_j \in R} \frac{link(k_i \cap r_j)}{link(k_i)} \right]}{\sum_{k_i \in K} |k_i|}$$

where for any set S, $link(S)$ denotes the number of links between elements of S (so $link(S) = |S| \cdot (|S| - 1)/2$).

	Solution 1			Solution 2		
	R	P	F1	R	P	F1
MUC	0.60	1	0.74	0.60	1	0.74
B-cub	0.51	1	0.67	0.51	1	0.67
CEAFm	0.71	1	0.83	0.71	1	0.83
CEAFe	0.82	0.82	0.82	0.82	0.82	0.82
LEA	0.42	1	0.60	0.42	1	0.60
NEC	0.71	1	0.83	0	1	0

Table 2: Evaluation of the hypothetical examples in Table 1. NEC is the new metric introduced in Section 3.

The goal of NEC is to link all mentions referring to a named entity to the correct name. Consider the example in Table 1. There are two entities, each with one named mention and a few pronouns. Both solutions find the same number of correct mentions pairs. However, solution 1 has a named mention in each cluster but solution 2 has only pronouns. Standard evaluations have the same values for both solutions (see Table 2) because they do not consider the types of mentions.

3 NEC Evaluation Metrics

The above example highlights the potential deficiencies of standard coreference evaluations when applied to NEC. Here we introduce a set of task-specific criteria for the evaluation of NEC.[1]

3.1 NEC F1

In the gold-standard, all mentions to named entities are grouped into chains. We wish to find a chain corresponding to each entity in the system output also. To map chains between the gold-standard and the system output, we select for each gold-standard chain, the predicted chain that has the highest F1 score with respect to its mentions. The NEC F1 score is the average of these highest per entity scores.[2]

To compute the intersection between a gold-standard and a system chain, we first augment each gold-standard chain with a list of all variations of the entity's name. We rely on the gold-standard named entity annotation and intersect this with the membership in a coreference chain. This provides lists of the full name, last name, occasionally nicknames, i.e. {*Frank Curzio, Francis X. Curzio, Curzio*}, {*Dwayne Dog Chapman, Dog Chapman, Chapman*}. We consider a predicted chain to be a candidate match for a gold chain only if it contains at least one of the name variants. We do not use exact mention match to find candidate chains as the presence of the name can indicate which entity the cluster is about. If the gold mention is 'Mr Joe from Boston' and the system finds 'Mr Joe', we still consider the chain containing this mention to be a candidate chain as the name can be determined and other mentions may have been resolved correctly.

For each named entity $k_i \in K$, let N_i be the set of response mentions that contain the full name of k_i. For a key named entity k_i and a response entity r_j, the precision is defined to be $p(k_i, r_j) = \frac{|r_j \cap k_i|}{|r_j|}$ and the recall is defined to be $r(k_i, r_j) = \frac{|r_j \cap k_i|}{|k_i|}$. The $F1$ for this pair of key entity and response entity is then given by $f(k_i, r_j) = \frac{2p(k_i,r_j)r(k_i,r_j)}{p(k_i,r_j)+r(k_i,r_j)} = \frac{2|r_j \cap k_i|}{|r_j|+|k_i|}$. Then F1 for the key named entity k_i is

$$\text{F1}_i = \max_{r_j \in R: r_j \cap N_i \neq \emptyset} f(k_i, r_j)$$

We use an exact span matching between gold and predicted mentions to calculate F1 to be consistent with the existing scorers.

If a gold-standard chain does not get paired with any system chain, the F1 for that chain is taken to be zero. We find the overall F1 of the system as the average of the F1 for each gold chain, $\frac{1}{|K|} \sum_{k_i \in K} \text{F1}_i$.

3.2 Entity not Found

The NEC F1 gives a sense of overall performance but mixes true purity of the system-discovered entities and the ability to discover entities at all. "Entity not found" is the error when no NEC system output overlaps with a gold standard chain. These contribute a score of 0 for the average F1.[3]

3.3 Pronoun Resolution Accuracy

We also track the NEC F1 when only mentions of given syntactic type are preserved in the chain—name, pronoun and nominal. Of special interest is to track performance when resolving pronouns. Many of the errors on pronouns arise due to the need for common-sense knowledge and reasoning.

3.4 Over-Splitting/Combination of Entities

We tracked the over-splitting (systems produce multiple clusters for the same name) and the over-combination of entities as well (placing mentions to different named entities in the same cluster. This error usually occurs when different people have the same last name but also occasionally when the names are completely different but the roles of the people are similar. However, overall

[1] See supplementary material for examples of the errors.

[2] Although the task appears similar to Entity Linking (EL) (Mihalcea and Csomai, 2007; Ratinov et al., 2011), it does not involve linking an entity to a knowledge base (KB). Not all entities even need to be in a KB. Also, EL typically focuses on names and other nouns whereas coreference includes pronouns as well.

[3] We consider only chains containing a named mention. Chains that do not contain any named mention are filtered out. More details on filtering in section 4.

	PER			ORG			GPE		
	Chains not found	NEC F1	Coref F1	Chains not found	NEC F1	Coref F1	Chains not found	NEC F1	Coref F1
(Raghunathan et al., 2010)	16%	0.55	0.50	34%	0.42	0.41	14%	0.67	0.56
(Clark and Manning, 2015)	36%	0.46	0.56	40%	0.39	0.46	21%	0.61	0.61
(Clark and Manning, 2016a,b)	21%	0.61	0.67	29%	0.50	0.52	17%	0.68	0.65
(Lee et al., 2017)	28%	0.58	0.69	26%	0.58	0.56	12%	0.76	0.68
(Lee et al., 2018)	7.5%	0.80	0.77	15%	0.69	0.61	8%	0.81	0.69

Table 3: Performance of systems. Chains not found and NEC F1 refer to the new named entity focused metrics. Coref F1 refers to the evaluation combining MUC, B^3 and CEAFE, on test data.

	PER			ORG			GPE		
	Name	Pronoun	Nominal	Name	Pronoun	Nominal	Name	Pronoun	Nominal
(Raghunathan et al., 2010)	0.55	0.45	0.23	0.47	0.35	0.11	0.73	0.44	0.19
(Clark and Manning, 2015)	0.50	0.34	0.10	0.46	0.34	0.15	0.65	0.57	0.22
(Clark and Manning, 2016a,b)	0.66	0.49	0.15	0.54	0.47	0.33	0.72	0.59	0.41
(Lee et al., 2017)	0.64	0.41	0.15	0.65	0.48	0.39	0.80	0.70	0.47
(Lee et al., 2018)	0.85	0.58	0.26	0.76	0.64	0.47	0.85	0.77	0.51

Table 4: NEC F1 by type of mention. The errors on names are high, though it is possible to resolve these with NER and string matching or similarity. Pronoun errors are high as expected.

such errors were quite small and similar for all systems and have thus not been included in the later tables with results.

4 Evaluation of Systems

We make use of the relevant part of OntoNotes coreference corpus (Pradhan et al., 2007) and gold-standard annotations for named entities on the same data to quantify the patterns in coreference of different named entity types (see the table in the supplementary material) and to evaluate systems on the newswire, broadcast news and magazine documents for PER, ORG and GPE entities.

Patterns in Coreference Named people, organizations and locations make up 38% of all coreference clusters in OntoNotes (Pradhan et al., 2007), yet 54% of all mentions that require coreference resolution are mentions of these types. All named entities are on average much less likely to be singletons than a typical entity, mentioned only once in the text and not requiring coreference resolution (De Marneffe et al., 2015). People, organizations and locations are most likely to be mentioned repeatedly: 68% of people, 51% of organizations and 52% of locations named in text have at least one other coreferent mention to them.

Named entities have a large portion of references that are not by name. Nominals account for less than 5% of the mentions in all genres for PER, while the remaining mentions are split almost equally between names and pronouns. For ORG, roughly half of the mentions are named, the remaining are equally split between pronouns and nominals. For GPE, roughly 70% of the mentions are named and others are mostly pronouns.

Systems We evaluate the Stanford coreference system, with its deterministic (Raghunathan et al., 2010; Lee et al., 2011; Recasens et al., 2013), statistical (Clark and Manning, 2015) and neural (Clark and Manning, 2016a,b) versions, and the neural end-to-end systems of (Lee et al., 2017) and (Lee et al., 2018) on traditional and NEC metrics.

These general coreference systems find coreferring expressions of any type and produce coreference chains for all mentioned entities. In NEC, the goal is to find all mentions to *an entity* that has been *referred to by name* at least once in the document. The output of off-the-shelf coreference systems has to be filtered to keep only chains that contain at least one mention noun phrase with a syntactic head that is a entity's name.[4] For our evaluation, we use the spaCy dependency parsing system (Honnibal and Johnson, 2015) to detect whether a name is the head of a mention, by checking that no other word in the mention is an ancestor of the name in the dependency parse tree. In evaluation, we use gold NER tags to determine if the head is a name. Note that the dependency parsing and gold NER are not given to the systems but are used to process their output.

Many system NEC chains did not have any

[4]Less strict filtering, such as the presence of an appropriate pronoun could also indicate that it a specific type of entity. For NEC, we insist on having at least one named mention.

named mentions. (Lee et al., 2017) does not have a named mention in about 30% of the coreference chains on PER that do contain a personal or possessive third person pronoun. This number is about 20% for the CoreNLP neural system.

Table 3 shows the standard and NEC F1 on all the systems. For PER, there are three notable leaps of improvement according to the standard coref evaluation: between the statistical and rule-based CoreNLP systems, between their statistical and neural systems and between the two versions of the AllenNLP systems. Some of these improvements contradict actual performance on NEC, notably for the difference between the rule-based and statistical systems. The other two improvements in Coref F1 translate to improvements in NEC metrics. The difference between the statistical and rule-based system is also falsely reflected in standard F1 for ORG and ORG entities. As expected, (Lee et al., 2018) outperforms all the systems, with (Lee et al., 2017) as a close second. Both perform much better than (Raghunathan et al., 2010) and (Clark and Manning, 2015). (Clark and Manning, 2016a,b) does slightly better than (Lee et al., 2017) on PER entities. Notably, (Lee et al., 2018) misses less than 10% of the chains for all entity types compared to 20-40% by other systems.

Note that the performance varies considerably across entity types. A top NER system such as (Ratinov and Roth, 2009) that focus on PER, ORG and GPE does not find a single named entity in just 4.67%, 5.7% and 1.1% of chains respectively. However, the percentage of chains not found is much higher. It is possible that the non-named mentions were resolved to each other but not to any names so such chains got filtered out for the NEC task. Future work involves developing coreference systems driven by NER and producing results more suitable for downstream tasks.

We also separate the performance of the systems by mention type. The second panel of Table 3 reveals that (Lee et al., 2018) outperforms all the systems on each mention type for all the three types of entities. Detection of named mentions can be done with high accuracy by named entity recognition systems (Stoyanov et al., 2009) and the matching of names can also be done accurately via string matching (Wacholder et al., 1997; Wick et al., 2009). In spite of this, most systems do not perform well on names. The mistakes on pronouns and nominals are much higher as expected.

While (Lee et al., 2018) gets a better F1 on the standard coreference metrics used as well, it improves on many aspects of performance. It finds more chains and even performs better resolution of each mention type, making it more suitable for downstream tasks.

5 Conclusion

We presented the task of Named Entity Coreference (NEC) and argued that the standard coreference metrics are not suitable for the evaluation of this task. We introduced evaluation metrics that tackle the shortcomings of the standard metrics for the task and track the different errors made by systems. We showed that many off-the-shelf systems do not perform well on these metrics. They output many clusters without a link to any name or a link to the incorrect name, making results unsuitable for downstream applications. Our metrics track different aspects of system performance and help identify such issues.

Acknowledgments

This work was supported in part by Contract HR0011-15-2-0025 with the US Defense Advanced Research Projects Agency (DARPA). The views expressed are those of the authors and do not reflect the official policy or position of the Department of Defense or the U.S. Government.

References

Amit Bagga and Breck Baldwin. 1998. Entity–based cross–document coreferencing using the vector space model. In *36th Annual Meeting of the Association for Computational Linguistics and 17th International Conference on Computational Linguistics, COLING-ACL '98, Université de Montréal, Montréal, Quebec, Canada. Proceedings of the Conference*, pages 79–85.

Chen Chen and Vincent Ng. 2013. Linguistically aware coreference evaluation metrics. In *Proceedings of the Sixth International Joint Conference on Natural Language Processing*, pages 1366–1374.

Kevin Clark and Christopher D Manning. 2015. Entity-centric coreference resolution with model stacking. In *Proceedings of the 53rd Annual Meeting of the Association for Computational Linguistics and the 7th International Joint Conference on Natural Language Processing (Volume 1: Long Papers)*, pages 1405–1415.

Kevin Clark and Christopher D Manning. 2016a. Deep reinforcement learning for mention-ranking coreference models. In *Proceedings of the 2016 Conference on Empirical Methods in Natural Language Processing*, pages 2256–2262.

Kevin Clark and Christopher D Manning. 2016b. Improving coreference resolution by learning entity-level distributed representations. In *Proceedings of the 54th Annual Meeting of the Association for Computational Linguistics (Volume 1: Long Papers)*, pages 643–653.

Marie-Catherine De Marneffe, Marta Recasens, and Christopher Potts. 2015. Modeling the lifespan of discourse entities with application to coreference resolution. *J. Artif. Int. Res.*, 52(1):445–475.

Matthew Honnibal and Mark Johnson. 2015. An improved non-monotonic transition system for dependency parsing. In *Proceedings of the 2015 Conference on Empirical Methods in Natural Language Processing*, pages 1373–1378, Lisbon, Portugal. Association for Computational Linguistics.

Heng Ji and Ralph Grishman. 2011. Knowledge base population: Successful approaches and challenges. In *Proceedings of the 49th Annual Meeting of the Association for Computational Linguistics: Human Language Technologies – Volume 1*, HLT '11, pages 1148–1158.

Heeyoung Lee, Yves Peirsman, Angel Chang, Nathanael Chambers, Mihai Surdeanu, and Dan Jurafsky. 2011. Stanford's multi-pass sieve coreference resolution system at the conll-2011 shared task. In *Proceedings of the 15th conference on computational natural language learning: Shared task*, pages 28–34. Association for Computational Linguistics.

Kenton Lee, Luheng He, Mike Lewis, and Luke Zettlemoyer. 2017. End-to-end neural coreference resolution. In *Proceedings of the 2017 Conference on Empirical Methods in Natural Language Processing*, pages 188–197.

Kenton Lee, Luheng He, and Luke Zettlemoyer. 2018. Higher–order coreference resolution with coarse–to–fine inference. In *Proceedings of the 2018 Conference of the North American Chapter of the Association for Computational Linguistics: Human Language Technologies, Volume 2 (Short Papers)*, pages 687–692.

Xiaoqiang Luo. 2005. On coreference resolution performance metrics. In *HLT/EMNLP 2005, Human Language Technology Conference and Conference on Empirical Methods in Natural Language Processing, Proceedings of the Conference, Vancouver, British Columbia, Canada*, pages 25–32.

Gideon S Mann. 2002. Fine–grained proper noun ontologies for question answering. In *Proceedings of the 2002 workshop on Building and using semantic networks–Volume 11*, pages 1–7. Association for Computational Linguistics.

Sebastian Martschat and Michael Strube. 2014. Recall error analysis for coreference resolution. In *Proceedings of the 2014 Conference on Empirical Methods in Natural Language Processing (EMNLP)*, pages 2070–2081.

Rada Mihalcea and Andras Csomai. 2007. Wikify!: Linking documents to encyclopedic knowledge.

Nafise Sadat Moosavi and Michael Strube. 2016. Which coreference evaluation metric do you trust? a proposal for a link-based entity aware metric. In *Proceedings of the 54th Annual Meeting of the Association for Computational Linguistics (Volume 1: Long Papers)*, pages 632–642.

Sameer Pradhan, Xiaoqiang Luo, Marta Recasens, Eduard Hovy, Vincent Ng, and Michael Strube. 2014. Scoring coreference partitions of predicted mentions: A reference implementation. In *Proceedings of the 52nd Annual Meeting of the Association for Computational Linguistics (Volume 2: Short Papers)*, pages 30–35, Baltimore, Maryland. Association for Computational Linguistics.

Sameer S Pradhan, Eduard Hovy, Mitch Marcus, Martha Palmer, Lance Ramshaw, and Ralph Weischedel. 2007. Ontonotes: A unified relational semantic representation. *International Journal of Semantic Computing*, 1(04):405–419.

Karthik Raghunathan, Heeyoung Lee, Sudarshan Rangarajan, Nathanael Chambers, Mihai Surdeanu, Dan Jurafsky, and Christopher Manning. 2010. A multi-pass sieve for coreference resolution. In *Proceedings of the 2010 Conference on Empirical Methods in Natural Language Processing*, pages 492–501. Association for Computational Linguistics.

L. Ratinov and D. Roth. 2009. Design challenges and misconceptions in named entity recognition. In *CoNLL*, pages 147–155.

Lev Ratinov, Dan Roth, Doug Downey, and Mike Anderson. 2011. Local and global algorithms for disambiguation to wikipedia. In *Proc. of the Annual Meeting of the Association for Computational Linguistics (ACL)*.

Marta Recasens, Marie-Catherine de Marneffe, and Christopher Potts. 2013. The life and death of discourse entities: Identifying singleton mentions. In *Proceedings of the 2013 Conference of the North American Chapter of the Association for Computational Linguistics: Human Language Technologies*, pages 627–633.

Veselin Stoyanov, Nathan Gilbert, Claire Cardie, and Ellen Riloff. 2009. Conundrums in noun phrase coreference resolution: Making sense of the state–of–the–art. In *ACL 2009, Proceedings of the 47th Annual Meeting of the Association for Computational Linguistics and the 4th International Joint Conference on Natural Language Processing of the AFNLP, Singapore*, pages 656–664.

Marc Vilain, John Burger, John Aberdeen, Dennis Connolly, and Lynette Hirschman. 1995. A model–theoretic coreference scoring scheme. In *Proceedings of the 6th Conference on Message Understanding*, MUC6 '95, pages 45–52.

Nina Wacholder, Yael Ravin, and Misook Choi. 1997. Disambiguation of proper names in text. In *Proceedings of the Fifth Conference on Applied Natural Language Processing*, ANLC '97, pages 202–208.

Kellie Webster, Marta Recasens, Vera Axelrod, and Jason Baldridge. 2018. Mind the gap: A balanced corpus of gendered ambiguous pronouns. *Transactions of the Association for Computational Linguistics*, 6:605–617.

Robert West, Evgeniy Gabrilovich, Kevin Murphy, Shaohua Sun, Rahul Gupta, and Dekang Lin. 2014. Knowledge base completion via search-based question answering. In *Proceedings of the 23rd international conference on World wide web*, pages 515–526. ACM.

Michael Wick, Aron Culotta, Khashayar Rohanimanesh, and Andrew McCallum. 2009. An entity based model for coreference resolution. In *Proceedings of the 2009 SIAM International Conference on Data Mining*, pages 365–376. SIAM.

Liang Zhou, Miruna Ticrea, and Eduard Hovy. 2004. Multi–document biography summarization. In *Proceedings of the 2004 Conference on Empirical Methods in Natural Language Processing*.

Neural Coreference Resolution with Limited Lexical Context and Explicit Mention Detection for Oral French

Loïc Grobol
Lattice CNRS, 1 rue Maurice Arnoux, 92120 Montrouge, France
ALMAnaCH, Inria, 2 rue Simone Iff, 75589 Paris, France
loic.grobol@inria.fr

Abstract

We propose an end-to-end coreference resolution system obtained by adapting neural models that have recently improved the state-of-the-art on the OntoNotes benchmark to make them applicable to other paradigms for this task. We report the performances of our system on ANCOR, a corpus of transcribed oral French — for which it constitutes a new baseline with proper evaluation.

1 Introduction

In the last few years, coreference resolution systems based on artificial neural networks architectures have received much attention by tremendously improving upon the previous state-of-the-art. In particular, the system introduced by K. Lee et al. (2017) and refined in (K. Lee et al. 2018) have proved that relatively high scores could be achieved without relying on rich features and preprocessing pipelines.

However, these results were obtained in the paradigm of the CoNLL-2012 shared task (Pradhan et al. 2012) and it is not self-evident that they are generalisable to other datasets, other domains and other languages. For instance, the choice in to not include singleton mentions in the CoNLL-2012 dataset is quite uncommon and might rightfully be suspected to affect the evaluation of coreference resolution architectures (see for instance the comparisons made by Poesio et al. (2018)).

In this work, we present an adaptation of K. Lee et al. (2018)'s system (henceforth E2EC[1]) to make it more suitable to other paradigms. We evaluate our system on ANCOR (Muzerelle et al. 2014) — a corpus of transcribed oral French.

[1]From its official repository `https://github.com/kentonl/e2e-coref`.

2 Related Works

There is a large existing body of work on coreference resolution spanning from the 1970s of which Poesio et al. (2016) provides an exhaustive review. In recent years, the field has been dominated by machine learning approaches — with the notable exception of the rule-based system of H. Lee et al. (2013) — from shallow learning approaches (C. Ma et al. 2014; Björkelund and Kuhn 2014; Durrett and Klein 2014) to systems based on artificial neural network architectures (Clark and Manning 2016a; Clark and Manning 2016b; Wiseman et al. 2015; Wiseman et al. 2016), gradually reducing their dependency on rich features coming from preprocessing pipelines using linguistic knowledge. One of the last incarnations of this tendency is the E2EC system introduced by K. Lee et al. (2017), which has close to no dependency to external resources (except for pretrained word embeddings derived from non-annotated data) and yet reaches state-of-the-art performance on the most common benchmark: the fully end-to-end track of the CoNLL-2012 shared task (Pradhan et al. 2012).

At the core of E2EC is the idea of performing coreference detection on the set of all possible text spans instead of using markables detected by an independent mention detector. This is made possible through the use of dense representations of arbitrary text spans derived from the internal states of recurrent neural networks. K. Lee et al. (2018) introduced further improvements to this model, most notably a higher-order approach to coreference detection using incremental refinements of its spans representations based on their antecedent distributions and an early pruning of antecedent candidates based on a coarse-to-fine scoring strategy.

However, to the best of our knowledge, using a simple classifier on these span embeddings to detect mentions had not yet been explored. Even

Proceedings of the 2nd Workshop on Computational Models of Reference, Anaphora and Coreference (CRAC 2019), pages 8–14,
Minneapolis, USA, June 7, 2019.

Sanh et al. (2018) — which used the AllenNLP (Gardner et al. 2018) implementation of E2EC for the coreference detection part of its system — used a sequence labelling-based model for entity-mention detection instead.

On our target corpus, ANCOR (Muzerelle et al. 2014), there have been relatively few works focused on automatic coreference resolution. Désoyer et al. (2015) presented an exploration of shallow learning techniques for the coreference detection phase, using the rich features provided by the gold annotations, delegating to further works the task of automatically detecting these features for a full-end-to-end pipeline. Some exploratory work on detecting mentions and these features has been presented in Grobol et al. (2017) with encouraging but limited results. The independent work presented by Godbert and Favre (2017) treated coreference resolution with a rule-based system on top of the MACAON pipeline (Nasr et al. 2011), focusing on pronominal anaphora resolution, yet reaching encouraging overall performances.

3 Model

Our architecture is mostly an adaptation of the version of E2EC presented by K. Lee et al. (2018), modified to address the difficulty of applying it to other paradigms, which is mainly due to two factors. The first one is that E2EC always operate at the level of a whole document. In principle, this would be a desirable property, since coreference chains are document-level objects. However, during the training process, it implies that the whole document has to be kept in memory and that error backpropagation must span all of its processing, which results in impractical memory and computing requirements. K. Lee et al. (2017) address this by performing a variety of aggressive pruning at every step, which complexifies its implementation and makes the training process less efficient. Despite this, the final implementation is still quite demanding in resources, particularly with huge documents and not necessarily effective on data — like ANCOR— where the context outside of the immediate vicinity of a span might be very noisy. It also prevents the use of common training techniques, like mini-batching and sample shuffling, since it imposes the use of batches that are each the size of a whole document.

The second characteristic we address is the lack of explicit mention detection. E2EC does not make a distinction between non-mention text spans and singleton mentions and as such, does not actually perform mention detection[2]. This is not a real problem on CoNLL-2012, but it is one for corpora that include singleton mentions. It also prevents the use of gold mentions to evaluate the actual coreference detection capabilities of a system without the bias induced by mention detection.

To alleviate these issue, our system are then should only take into account the immediate context of text spans rather than whole documents and that perform mention detection as an explicit step in order to take singleton mentions into account. In addition to these adaptations, we also added a certain number of incremental modifications inspired from recent works on sequence embeddings in neural networks. These modifications were added during our initial experiments on the mention detection part, for which they improved the global scores on the development dataset, but at the time of writing, we did not assess their actual impact on the whole architecture.

Words representations Similarly to e.g. X. Ma and Hovy (2016), we use a combination of pretrained word embeddings and character-level encodings derived from a recurrent neural layer (in our case a bidirectional GRU (Cho et al. 2014)), which helps with noisy inputs (including disfluencies, incomplete words and typos in ANCOR) but also unknown words and casing information that is not available to the pretrained word embeddings.

Span embeddings The span embeddings are computed using a combination of recurrent and self-attentional mechanisms. At the core is a bidirectional LSTM with two layers, that we run on the sequence of the representations $(w_{-\ell}, \dots, w_0, \dots, w_{n-1}, w_n, \dots, w_{n+p})$ of the words of the span (from w_0 to w_{n-1}) and its immediate left and right contexts. We keep the hidden states $h_i = [\overleftarrow{h_i}, \overrightarrow{h_i}]$ of both directions of the top LSTM layer, and use them in three subsequent treatments

- The hidden states of the first and the last word of the span are kept as a pure recurrent representation $r = [h_0, h_{n-1}]$
- The self-attention soft-head mechanism introduced by K. Lee et al. (2017) is applied to the sequence $([w_0, h_0], \dots [w_{n-1}, h_{n-1}])$ with

[2] It does compute a "mention score", but more as way to reduce the computational complexity of the architecture than as an explicit mention detection, and the correlation between this score and "mentionity" of text spans has not yet been studied.

two separate heads (inspired by the multi-head attention mechanism of Vaswani et al. (2017)) whose concatenation gives us an attentional representation a

- The final states of the LSTM are kept as a representation of the span context $c=[\overrightarrow{h_{-\ell}},\overleftarrow{h_{n+p}}]$. This was not part of the initial model, but we found that it helps significantly (at least for mention detection) on the most interactive parts of ANCOR.

The final span embedding s is then obtained by concatenating these three representations and f, a low-dimension feature embedding that encodes the length of the span and passing the result through a feedforward network giving $s=\mathrm{FFNN}_{\mathrm{out}}(r,a,c,f)$.

Mentions detection The mention detecting layer is a simple feedforward classifier that takes s as input and outputs a vector of class scores: "None" for non-mention spans and depending on the corpus, either a simple "NP" class for all mentions or distinct classes for noun phrases and pronouns.

Antecedents scoring The antecedent scoring layer assign coreference scores to mention/antecedent pairs using the same coarse-to-fine second-order inference mechanism as E2EC, with the representation refining done solely for the mention and not its antecedents. The only other variation is that instead of fixing the score of the dummy antecedent ε for a span s to 0 we instead compute a specific mention-new score by applying a simple feedforward network on s. This was motivated by the higher number of non-anaphoric mentions in ANCOR (again due to the inclusion of singleton mentions) and seems to affect the final coreference scores positively, although a more formal assessment of this is still needed.

4 Evaluation

Following the recommendations of Recasens (2010, p. 122) and Salmon-Alt et al. (2004) we evaluate our system separately on the two subtasks that it performs. For mention detection, we report the usual Precision, Recall and F-score detection metrics. For coreference resolution, we use the CoNLL-2012 metrics (Pradhan et al. 2014) including BLANC (Recasens and Hovy 2011). This is a standard evaluation procedure for coreference resolution systems — as seen for example in the CRAC18 shared task (Poesio et al. 2018). It also allows us to compare our system with other works on ANCOR (Désoyer et al. 2015; Godbert and Favre 2017) and to assess the actual capabilities of our antecedent scoring module by avoiding the noise caused by the inevitable mention detection errors.

5 Experiments

5.1 Data

The primary object of our study is the ANCOR corpus (Muzerelle et al. 2014). ANCOR is, for now, the only currently publicly available[3] corpus of French with coreference annotations whose size is sufficient for machine learning purposes, with around 418 000 words. The source materials of this corpus are *speech transcriptions*[4] , in most part long interviews with low interactivity taken from the ESLO corpus (Baude and Dugua 2011) and smaller parts with higher interactivity[5]. Its annotations include coreference and morphosyntactic annotations for noun phrases and pronouns including singleton mentions, but no linguistic annotations of other elements.

Since existing works on ANCOR do not provide detailed training/development/test partitions, ours is probably different, but we tried to stay reasonably close to the one described by Désoyer et al. (2015), with about 60 % of the corpus devoted to the training set. However, we chose to keep most of the rest to the test set, in order to provide more significant final scores. The final distribution is 59 %/12 %/29 %, with a fairly homogeneous distribution of the different subcorpora, in order to minimize the disparities caused by their various levels of interactivity and topics.

5.2 Hyperparameters

In order to stay close to the original E2EC model, we have mostly kept the same hyperparameters and mention here only those that we changed. All of these changes were motivated by purely empirical observations of the performance of the model on the ANCOR development set.

[3]Another large scale corpus exists (Tutin et al. 2000) but is not publicly available.

[4]The fact that the source material is not written (or controlled oral) language — as in most coreference corpora— is another factor that might skew the comparison with other works, but assessing its actual impact would require a comparable corpus for written French, which does not exist yet.

[5]See Brassier et al. (2018) for details on this part.

Table 1: Coreference resolution

System	MUC			B^3			$CEAF_e$			CoNLL	BLANC		
	P	R	F	P	R	F	P	R	F	Avg.	P	R	F
Désoyer et al. (2015)	—	—	63.5	—	—	83.8	—	—	79.0	75.3	—	—	67.4
Godbert and Favre (2017)	—	—	—	—	—	—	—	—	—	—	—	—	65.7[1]
Our model[2]	72.3	47.7	57.3	89.7	71.0	79.2	72.8	86.0	79.4	72.0	78.2	60.1	65.7

[1] It is not clear if the score reported as BLANC by Godbert and Favre (2017) actually takes into account both coreference and non-coreference links after rebuilding mention clusters or is simply the raw F-score of the antecedent finder.
[2] Averages on 5 runs.

Words representations We use word embeddings pretrained on the Common Crawl for FastText (Grave et al. 2018) and fine-tuned during training. The character embeddings are not pretrained and are initialized randomly.

Span encoding The span contexts considered are of size 10 on both sides. We only consider spans of at most 25 words to reduce the time and material requirements. Experiments made with longer spans did not show significantly different results. Our hypothesis is that too few mentions are longer than this limit to impact the learning.

Antecedent scoring During the antecedent scoring phase, only the 100 previous mentions are considered for coarse scoring and only the 25 best-scoring antecedents are kept for fine-scoring.

Training We trained the network sequentially, first on mention detection, then on antecedent scoring. For both, the trainable parameters were optimized using the AdamW (Loshchilov and Hutter 2019) optimizer.

For mention detection, we minimize the class-weighted cross-entropy (Panchapagesan et al. 2016) with a weight of 1 for "None" and 3 for the mention span class. We also undersample the spans in the training set to a maximum ratio of 90 % of non-mention spans, to alleviate the usual issues of neural classifiers with severe classes imbalance. For antecedent scoring, we follow K. Lee et al. (2017) and optimize the sum of the log-likelihood of all the correct antecedents of each mention.

5.3 Results

Mention detection Table 2 presents the results of our experiments with mention detection compared to the baseline of Grobol et al. (2017) — which consists in merely extracting all the NP from the output of an off-the-shelf parser — and the performance reported by Godbert and Favre (2017). Considering the sparsity of its own resources, our system does not fare too bad, even though its precision shows a lot of room for improvements.

Table 2: Mention detection

System	P	R	F
Grobol et al. (2017)	57.28	77.07	65.72
Godbert and Favre (2017)	90.05	87.86	88.94
Our model[1]	82.99	89.07	85.87

[1] Averages on 5 runs.

Coreference resolution Table 1 presents the performances of our system for coreference resolution and compare it with those of previous works. Note that we didn't compare with the performances of the original E2EC on ANCOR, since there is no simple way to provide it with gold mentions[6] at either training or test time, nor to make it distinguish between singleton mention and non-mention spans without significantly modifying it.

As mentioned in the previous sections, the existing work on ANCOR have been developed in different paradigms and as such are not entirely comparable to ours. This is particularly true for Désoyer et al. (2015), which relies on gold features, and as such was able to get very high scores on all metrics with a relatively simple system, these results should thus be considered as an upper baseline than a real benchmark. In addition, none of these works report the full detailed CoNLL-2012 metrics, which limits the interpretability of these results. Taking these reserves into account the performances of

[6] In the usual sense and not in the "anaphoric gold mentions" sense used in K. Lee et al. (2017).

our system suggests that neural architectures can indeed be effective in the paradigm of ANCOR.

6 Conclusion

We presented an end-to-end coreference resolution system inspired by the most recent models to reach state-of-the-art performance on the classic CoNLL-2012/Ontonotes dataset. Our system is made suitable for experiments on other datasets by the extraction of an explicit mention detection phase from the original end-to-end architecture of K. Lee et al. (2017) and the restriction of the input representations to the immediate contexts of the markables. Given these adaptations, we report performances on ANCOR — a corpus of transcribed oral French— that are close to those reported by previous works, which required the use of considerably more linguistic knowledge.

This tends to prove that knowledge-poor, end-to-end neural architectures are applicable to coreference detection tasks beyond the OntoNotes benchmark. It also provides future works on coreference resolution for French with a baseline for full evaluations on both parts of the task.

However, our system has only been tested on a single corpus so far, and its architecture is optimized for it. Further assessment of its capabilities should include further tests on other, comparable, corpora such as ARRAU (Poesio and Artstein 2008), the Polish Coreference Corpus (Ogrodniczuk et al. 2016) or the upcoming DEMOCRAT corpus (Landragin 2016). Proper evaluation should also eventually include comparisons on the CoNLL-2012 dataset itself, possibly in the "gold mention boundaries" settings for a better comparability.

Acknowledgements

This work is part of the "Investissements d'Avenir" overseen by the French National Research Agency ANR-10-LABX-0083 (Labex EFL), and is also supported by the ANR DEMOCRAT (Describing and Modelling Reference Chains: Tools for Corpus Annotation and Automatic Processing) project ANR-15-CE38-0008.

References

Olivier Baude and Céline Dugua. 2011. (Re)faire le corpus d'Orléans quarante ans après : quoi de neuf, linguiste ? *Corpus*. Varia, 10, 2011: 99–118.

Anders Björkelund and Jonas Kuhn. 2014. Learning Structured Perceptrons for Coreference Resolution with Latent Antecedents and Non-Local Features. In *Proceedings of the 52nd Annual Meeting of the Association for Computational Linguistics*, pages 47–57. Volume 1. Association for Computational Linguistics.

Maëlle Brassier, Alexis Puret, Augustin Voisin-Marras, and Loïc Grobol. 2018. Classification par paires de mention pour la résolution des coréférences en français parlé interactif. In *Actes de la Conférence jointe CORIA-TALN-RJC 2018*. Association pour le Traitement Automatique des Langues. Rennes, France.

Kyunghyun Cho, Bart van Merrienboer, Caglar Gulcehre, Dzmitry Bahdanau, Fethi Bougares, Holger Schwenk, and Yoshua Bengio. 2014. Learning Phrase Representations Using RNN Encoder–Decoder for Statistical Machine Translation. In *Proceedings of the 2014 Conference on Empirical Methods in Natural Language Processing (EMNLP)*, pages 1724–1734. Association for Computational Linguistics.

Kevin Clark and Christopher D. Manning. 2016a. Deep Reinforcement Learning for Mention-Ranking Coreference Models. In *Proceedings of the 2016 Conference on Empirical Methods in Natural Language Processing, EMNLP 2016, Austin, Texas, USA, November 1-4, 2016*, pages 2256–2262.

Kevin Clark and Christopher D. Manning. 2016b. Improving Coreference Resolution by Learning Entity-Level Distributed Representations. In *Proceedings of the 54th Annual Meeting of the Association for Computational Linguistics*. Volume 1. Association for Computational Linguistics. Berlin, Deutschland.

Adèle Désoyer, Frédéric Landragin, Isabelle Tellier, Anaïs Lefeuvre, and Jean-Yves Antoine. 2015. Coreference Resolution for Oral Corpus: a machine learning experiment with ANCOR corpus. *Traitement Automatique des Langues*. Traitement automatique du langage parlé, 55.2, May 2015: 97–121.

Greg Durrett and Dan Klein. 2014. A Joint Model for Entity Analysis: Coreference, Typing, and Linking. *Transactions of the Association for Computational Linguistics*, 2.0, Nov. 1, 2014: 477–490.

Matt Gardner et al. 2018. AllenNLP: A Deep Semantic Natural Language Processing Platform.

In *Proceedings of Workshop for NLP Open Source Software*, pages 1–6. Association for Computational Linguistics.

Elisabeth Godbert and Benoît Favre. 2017. Détection de coréférences de bout en bout en français. In *Actes de la 24e Conférence sur le Traitement Automatique des Langues Naturelles*. Association pour le Traitement Automatique des Langues. Orléans, France.

Edouard Grave, Piotr Bojanowski, Prakhar Gupta, Armand Joulin, and Tomas Mikolov. 2018. Learning Word Vectors for 157 Languages. In *Proceedings of the 11th International Conference on Language Resources and Evaluation*. European Language Resource Association.

Loïc Grobol, Isabelle Tellier, Éric De La Clergerie, Marco Dinarelli, and Frédéric Landragin. 2017. Apports des analyses syntaxiques pour la détection automatique de mentions dans un corpus de français oral. In *Actes de la 24e Conférence sur le Traitement Automatique des Langues Naturelles*. Association pour le Traitement Automatique des Langues. Orléans, France.

Frédéric Landragin. 2016. Description, Modélisation et Détection Automatique Des Chaînes de Référence (DEMOCRAT). *Bulletin de l'AFIA*, 92, 2016: 11–15.

Heeyoung Lee, Angel Chang, Yves Peirsman, Nathanael Chambers, Mihai Surdeanu, and Dan Jurafsky. 2013. Deterministic Coreference Resolution Based on Entity-Centric, Precision-Ranked Rules. *Computational Linguistics*, 39.4, Dec. 2013: 885–916.

Kenton Lee, Luheng He, Mike Lewis, and Luke Zettlemoyer. 2017. End-to-End Neural Coreference Resolution. In *Proceedings of the 2017 Conference on Empirical Methods in Natural Language Processing*, pages 188–197. Association for Computational Linguistics. København, Danmark.

Kenton Lee, Luheng He, and Luke Zettlemoyer. 2018. Higher-Order Coreference Resolution with Coarse-to-Fine Inference. In *Proceedings of the 2018 Conference of the North American Chapter of the Association for Computational Linguistics: Human Language Technologies*, pages 687–692. Volume 2. Association for Computational Linguistics. New Orleans, Louisiana.

Ilya Loshchilov and Frank Hutter. 2019. Decoupled Weight Decay Regularization. In *International Conference on Learning Representations*. arXiv: 1711.05101.

Chao Ma, Janardhan Rao Doppa, J. Walker Orr, Prashanth Mannem, Xiaoli Fern, Tom Dietterich, and Prasad Tadepalli. 2014. Prune-and-Score: Learning for Greedy Coreference Resolution. In *Proceedings of the 2014 Conference on Empirical Methods in Natural Language Processing (EMNLP)*, pages 2115–2126. Association for Computational Linguistics.

Xuezhe Ma and Eduard Hovy. 2016. End-to-End Sequence Labeling via Bi-Directional LSTM-CNNs-CRF. In *Proceedings of the 54th Annual Meeting of the Association for Computational Linguistics*, pages 1064–1074. Volume 1. Association for Computational Linguistics. Berlin, Deutschland.

Judith Muzerelle, Anaïs Lefeuvre, Emmanuel Schang, Jean-Yves Antoine, Aurore Pelletier, Denis Maurel, Iris Eshkol, and Jeanne Villaneau. 2014. ANCOR Centre, a Large Free Spoken French Coreference Corpus: Description of the Resource and Reliability Measures. In *Proceedings of the Ninth International Conference on Language Resources and Evaluation*. European Language Resources Association. Reykjavík, Ísland.

Alexis Nasr, Frédéric Béchet, Jean-François Rey, Benoit Favre, and Joseph Le Roux. 2011. MACAON : An NLP Tool Suite for Processing Word Lattices. In *Proceedings of the 49th Annual Meeting of the Association for Computational Linguistics*, pages 86–91. United States.

Maciej Ogrodniczuk, Katarzyna Głowińska, Mateusz Kopeć, Agata Savary, and Magdalena Zawisławska. 2016. Polish Coreference Corpus. In Zygmunt Vetulani, Hans Uszkoreit, and Marek Kubis, editors, *Human Language Technology. Challenges for Computer Science and Linguistics*, pages 215–226. Lecture Notes in Computer Science. Springer International Publishing.

Sankaran Panchapagesan, Ming Sun, Aparna Khare, Spyros Matsoukas, Arindam Mandal, Björn Hoffmeister, and Shiv Vitaladevuni. 2016. Multi-Task Learning and Weighted Cross-Entropy for DNN-Based Keyword Spotting. In *Proceedings of Interspeech*, pages 760–764.

Massimo Poesio and Ron Artstein. 2008. Anaphoric Annotation in the ARRAU Corpus. In *Proceedings of the International Confer-*

ence on Language Resources and Evaluation. Marrakech, Morocco.

Massimo Poesio, Ron Stuckardt, and Yannick Versley. 2016. *Anaphora Resolution: Algorithms, Resources, and Applications*. Theory and Applications of Natural Language Processing. Springer Berlin Heidelberg.

Massimo Poesio et al. 2018. Anaphora Resolution with the ARRAU Corpus. In *Proceedings of the First Workshop on Computational Models of Reference, Anaphora and Coreference*, pages 11–22. Association for Computational Linguistics. New Orleans, Louisiana.

Sameer Pradhan, Xiaoqiang Luo, Marta Recasens, Eduard Hovy, Vincent Ng, and Michael Strube. 2014. Scoring Coreference Partitions of Predicted Mentions: A Reference Implementation. In *Proceedings of the 52nd Annual Meeting of the Association for Computational Linguistics*, pages 30–35. Volume 2. Association for Computational Linguistics. Baltimore, Maryland.

Sameer Pradhan, Alessandro Moschitti, Nianwen Xue, Olga Uryupina, and Yuchen Zhang. 2012. CoNLL-2012 Shared Task: Modeling Multilingual Unrestricted Coreference in OntoNotes. In *Proceedings of the Joint Conference on EMNLP and CoNLL*, pages 1–40. Association for Computational Linguistics. Jeju Island, Korea.

Marta Recasens. 2010. Coreference: Theory, Annotation, Resolution and Evaluation. Universitat de Barcelona, 2010.

Marta Recasens and Eduard Hovy. 2011. BLANC: Implementing the Rand Index for Coreference Evaluation. *Natural Language Engineering*, 17.4, Oct. 2011: 485–510.

Susanne Salmon-Alt, Laurent Romary, Andrei Popescu-Belis, and Loïs Rigouste. 2004. Online Evaluation of Coreference Resolution. In *4th International Conference on Language Resources and Evaluation*. European Language Resources Association. Lisboa, Portugal.

Victor Sanh, Thomas Wolf, and Sebastian Ruder. 2018. A Hierarchical Multi-Task Approach for Learning Embeddings from Semantic Tasks, Nov. 14, 2018: arXiv: `1811.06031 [cs]`.

Agnès Tutin, François Trouilleux, Catherine Clouzot, Éric Gaussier, Annie Zaenen, Stéphanie Rayot, and Georges Antoniadis. 2000. Annotating a Large Corpus with Anaphoric Links. In *Proceedings of the Third International Conference on Discourse Anaphora and Anaphora Resolution*. United Kingdom.

Ashish Vaswani, Noam Shazeer, Niki Parmar, Jakob Uszkoreit, Llion Jones, Aidan N Gomez, Łukasz Kaiser, and Illia Polosukhin. 2017. Attention Is All You Need. In I. Guyon, U. V. Luxburg, S. Bengio, H. Wallach, R. Fergus, S. Vishwanathan, and R. Garnett, editors, *Advances in Neural Information Processing Systems 30*, pages 5998–6008. Curran Associates, Inc. Long Beach, California.

Sam Wiseman, Alexander M. Rush, and Stuart M. Shieber. 2016. Learning Global Features for Coreference Resolution. In *Proceedings of the 2016 Conference of the North American Chapter of the Association for Computational Linguistics: Human Language Technologies*, pages 994–1004. Association for Computational Linguistics.

Sam Wiseman, Alexander M. Rush, Stuart M. Shieber, and Jason Weston. 2015. Learning Anaphoricity and Antecedent Ranking Features for Coreference Resolution. In *Proceedings of the 53rd Annual Meeting of the Association for Computational Linguistics and the 7th International Joint Conference on Natural Language Processing of the Asian Federation of Natural Language Processing*, pages 1416–1426. Volume 1. Beijing, China.

Entity Decisions in Neural Language Modelling: Approaches and Problems

Jenny Kunz and **Christian Hardmeier**
Department of Linguistics and Philology
Uppsala University
752 36 Uppsala, Sweden
jenny.kunz.7402@student.uu.se
christian.hardmeier@lingfil.uu.se

Abstract

We explore different approaches to explicit entity modelling in language models (LM). We independently replicate two existing models in a controlled setup, introduce a simplified variant of one of the models and analyze their performance in direct comparison. Our results suggest that today's models are limited as several stochastic variables make learning difficult. We show that the most challenging point in the systems is the decision if the next token is an entity token. The low precision and recall for this variable will lead to severe cascading errors. Our own simplified approach dispenses with the need for latent variables and improves the performance in the entity yes/no decision. A standard well-tuned baseline RNN-LM with a larger number of hidden units outperforms all entity-enabled LMs in terms of perplexity.

1 Introduction

Reference to entities in the world is a core feature of human language, and coreference between different mentions in a text is a fundamental property of coherent communication. Computational approaches to reference have long been studied in the area of coreference resolution (Ng, 2017). Very recently, explicit models of reference have also been studied in the context of language modelling. The usual approach is to introduce latent variables modelling whether the next token is part of an entity mention, and which of the previously seen entities it refers to.

In this work, we present a comparative study of three language modelling approaches with explicit representations of entity coreference: YangLM, the entity-enabled language model (LM) of Yang et al. (2016), the EntityNLM model of Ji et al. (2017), and SetLM, our own extension of the latter. YangLM and EntityNLM differ in the parameterization of the latent variables and the order in which decisions are made. SetLM is a simpler architecture with fewer loss functions. It replaces the latent variable modelling the decision whether to produce an entity with two extra embeddings, one for a new entity (similar to the other models) and one for the case that the token does not belong to an entity. We replicate the results of Yang et al. (2016) and Ji et al. (2017) with an independent reimplementation of their models in a comparable experimental setup and evaluate the models in terms of overall language modelling performance performance in comparison with a simple RNN-LM. We also study the accuracy and precision/recall in each individual decision step and look at the convergence of variables. We find that YangLM outperforms the other models in terms of perplexity, whereas SetLM achieves the best results for the entity yes/no prediction. None of the entity-enabled LMs is competitive with a simple RNN-LM having a higher number of hidden units, and we do not achieve similar gains by enlarging the hidden sizes of the entity LMs.

2 Approaches

RNNs for language modelling have been state of the art for a few years (Mikolov et al., 2013), mostly using LSTMs (Hochreiter and Schmidhuber, 1997; Sundermeyer et al., 2012). They model each token in a document based on their previous context:

$$h_t = LSTM(x_t h_{t-1}). \qquad (1)$$

The explicit incorporation of coreference in these LMs is a relatively new and less researched task. In the entity prediction process of such models, two fundamental decisions are made: (1) *Is the token (part of) an entity mention?* and (2) *Which entity does it refer to?* To our knowledge, Yang et al. (2016) were the first to implement this idea. In their model, (1) is handled with the variable z_t

Proceedings of the 2nd Workshop on Computational Models of Reference, Anaphora and Coreference (CRAC 2019), pages 15–19,
Minneapolis, USA, June 7, 2019.

for each position t with an attention mechanism (Bahdanau et al., 2014) with the LSTM hidden state over the set of observed entities h^e that also contains a learnable embedding e_{new} for a new entity that has not been observed yet. They estimate the probability distribution over the known entities and use the weighted sum for the decision whether the token is part of an entity mention.

$$p^{coref}(v_t|h^e, h_{t-1}) = ATTN(h^e, h_{t-1}) \quad (2)$$

$$d_t = \sum_{v_t} p(v_t) h^e_{v_t} \quad (3)$$

$$p(z_t|h_{t-1}) = sigmoid(W[h_{t-1}, d_t]) \quad (4)$$

If $z_t = 1$ (i.e. the word is an entity mention), the probability for the next word is calculated based on v_t (see Equation 2), the previous hidden state of the LSTM and the set h^e. If $z_t = 0$ then the next word is predicted based on the previous hidden state of the LSTM only.

EntityNLM (Ji et al., 2017) handles (1) with the variable R_t, corresponding to z_t, but in contrast to YangLM solely based on the LSTM hidden state, using a parametrized embedding associated with $r \in \{0, 1\}$. The decision which entity it refers to is handled with the variable $\mathrm{E_t}$ that denotes the index of the current entity in the set of known entities E_t in case $R_t = 1$, using the LSTM hidden state, the set of entities and a distance feature vector. The prediction of the next token x is always based on the LSTM hidden state h_{i1} and the representation of the current entity e even if it is not an entity. In this point EntityNLM also differs from YangLM that only uses the entity representation in the case that the token is predicted to be an entity token.

Ji et al. also introduce a length prediction variable L_t that is predicted when a new mention is started, using the last hidden state h_{t-1} and the most recent embedding of the entity e_t.

Clark et al. (2018) build on Ji et al. (2017) and track entities to use them as contextual information when generating narrative text. They evaluate their model in mention generation, sentence selection and sentence generation tasks, but not in the perplexity metric so that we cannot use their model for quantitative comparison.

Our SetLM model builds on YangLM and models each token in a document with an LSTM as above. It also saves the previously seen entities in a set, but instead of introducing a variable that controls if the next token is part of an entity mention or not, we include a learned embedding for the case that the token is not an entity token to the set, inspired by approaches in Question Answering with Answer Triggering (Zhao et al., 2017). The set E with the previously seen entities $e_1, ..., e_n$ has, besides e_{new} for the detection of a new entity, also contains the learnable embedding $e_{noentity}$ for the case that the token is not an entity. This makes it possible to dismiss the decision in Equation 4 in YangLM while keeping its remaining decision structure (Equation 1, 2 and 3).

The decision on the next token is, as in Yang et al.'s model, based on h_{t-1} and the corresponding embedding with the highest attention score in the set of entities if the token is part of a mention, and solely based on h_{t-1} otherwise.

3 Data

We train, optimize and evaluate the three models on the English subset of the OntoNotes 5.0 corpus (Weischedel et al., 2013) with 1.5 million words and anaphoric coreference annotation within a document, and use the CoNLL-2012 split into train, development and test set. We lowercased all tokens, replaced all numbers by a special symbol and all tokens with less than 5 occurrences with a special token for rare words, resulting in a vocabulary size of 11539. Like Ji et al. (2017), we keep only the embedding mentions where mentions are nested and removed all mention annotation where the mention length is higher than 25.

We did not reduce the length of the mentions in the data for YangLM to one as in the original model but use the setting as described above.

4 Implementation

We implemented all models in Python using the PyTorch deep learning library (Paszke et al., 2017). As candidate hyperparameters for the hidden size of the LSTM and word embedding layer, we tried the values 32, 48, 64, 128, 256, 512. We employ dropout (Srivastava et al., 2014) with candidate rates of 0.0, 0.1 or 0.2 and for the Adam optimizer (Kingma and Ba, 2014), we tried the learning rates 0.01, 0.005 and 0.001. We tried the models with GloVe (Pennington et al., 2014) and with randomly initialized, learnable word embeddings. We also experimented with a weighted loss with the intention to force the models to produce more entity mentions.

Based on the experimental results on the development set, we chose a hyperparameter setting for the model based on Yang et al. (2016) with 64 hidden units for both LSTM hidden size and word embedding size, Adam optimizer with $\lambda = 0.005$, a dropout rate of 0.2 and randomly initialized word embeddings. The model was trained for 20 epochs.

The best hyperparameter setting for the model based on EntityNLM was very similar and only differs in having a hidden size of 128 and being trained for 22 epochs. For SetLM, we chose a hidden size of 48 and 16 epochs.

For the evaluation of our main metric that is the token perplexity, we implement two baseline models that are purely LSTM-based LMs. We use the same architecture in two settings: one in the same hyperparameter setting as the best Yang et al. model with a hidden size of 64, trained for twelve epochs, and one optimized model with a hidden size of 512, trained for three epochs.

5 Evaluation

As the main metric for the language models general performance, we measure the perplexity. We also evaluate the entity prediction process qualitatively by measuring precision and recall for the question if the next token is part of an entity mention and the accuracy for the choice of the entity from the set, and evaluate the length prediction in the model based on EntityNLM. For our model, we regard the choice of $e_{noentity}$ as the *Entity No*-decision and the choice for either of the entities as the *Entity Yes*-decision. For the accuracy of the choice of the entity from the set, we only looked at the choices in the *Entity Yes*-case.

5.1 Perplexity

We report the results for our models and baselines on the test set along with the original results from Ji et al. (2017) in table 1.[1]

Based on these results, we cannot confirm that the models outperform a simple RNN-LM on the OntoNotes data set. Both RNN-LM baselines easily outperform both the re-implemented and the reported results of Ji et al. (2017), and the optimized baseline (RNN-512) also performs much better than the model based on Yang et al. (2016) and our model which though both outperform the RNN that has same hidden size as itself (RNN-64). The model based on Yang et al. clearly performs best among all entity-predicting models.

	All	**Ent.**	**Non-Ent.**
RNN-64	121	177	114
RNN-512	**96**	**126**	**88**
EntityNLM (rep.)	132	-	-
EntityNLM (own)	131	154	127
YangLM (own)	107	132	101
SetLM	114	154	108

Table 1: Token perplexity results

	Perplexity Ratio
RNN-64	0.68
RNN-512	0.76
YangLM (own)	0.81
EntityNLM (own)	**0.85**
SetLM	0.74

Table 2: Relation Perplexity All Tokens / Entity Tokens

The decision how to select a token seems to be generally harder on entity tokens in the data set as they generally and for all models have a higher perplexity than non-entity tokens. But measured by their overall performance, the entity tokens in the re-implemented EntityNLM and YangLM models are relatively better than in the other models, while SetLM lies between the baseline models. Table 2 shows the perplexity of all tokens divided by the perplexity of entity tokens only, giving a measure for the relative performance of the models on entity tokens. But these results must be seen with the constraint that EntityNLM and YangLM get access to gold entity lists, and that the perplexity is a metric that grows exponentially, which limits the comparability of the ratio. The fact that our model does not improve on entity tokens suggests that the improvements of the re-implemented EntityNLM and YangLM models are caused by the gold information.

5.2 Entity Prediction

As the models are optimized for perplexity, the following results would possibly have been better in other hyperparameter settings. We observed higher values on the development set during tuning and great oscillations of the scores for different

[1] Please note that we give the two re-implementations access to the correct entity lists at test time in order to be able to evaluate each of the decision steps independently. The original results by Ji et al. (2017) did not have this access to gold entity information, so that the results are not directly comparable. SetLM also comes without access to this information as the mention decisions are made in one step.

epochs which makes it hard to interpret specific results.

	Prec.	Recall	F1
YangLM (own)	**60.9%**	30.2%	40.3%
EntityNLM (own)	39.0%	53.9%	45.3%
SetLM	41.0%	**58.1%**	**48.1%**

Table 3: Entity Yes/No Prediction

Precision and recall of both models are low, suggesting that the question if the next word is an entity is highly challenging in a LM. SetLM has the highest F1 score, suggesting that the Entity Yes/No prediction is best handled without a discrete decision.

	Accuracy
YangLM (own)	65.8%
EntityNLM (own)	**67.8%**
SetLM	65.1%

Table 4: Entity Choice

The accuracy for the decision which entity to choose is comparatively high. The EntityNLM re-implementation obtains the best value with a substantial margin.

5.3 Length Prediction

The re-implementation of EntityNLM's length prediction is correct in 59.4% of all cases, with the average distance of the false predictions to the gold mention length being 2.85 tokens. The average lengths of the mentions in all three models differ only slightly, being 1.53 for the EntityNLM re-implementation, 1.43 for the Yang et al. re-implementation and 1.78 for SetLM. The average length in the Gold data is 2.25 tokens.

6 Discussion

While we cannot confirm that the incorporation of explicit entity information is helpful in a general language modelling task, and the models' abilities especially to predict where to form entities have shown to be limited, we see a potential for the continuous representations for entities to become better and to be useful in certain situations where entities re-appear over long distances, like in the narrative texts that were subject to Clark et al. (2018).

For short texts like in the OntoNotes data set, an RNN-based LM implicitly seems to learn enough information about entities and the error propagation caused by wrongly detected entities in the set and erroneous decisions in the prediction process outweigh the information gain compared to basing the decision on the hidden state only.

The models' results for the decision steps in the entity prediction process suggest that handling the question if the word belongs to an entity mention and which entity it is jointly with information from the set of entities is preferable over first deciding if the word belongs to an entity mention. The list of entities seems to be very helpful context for the question if the next word is an entity. As the question if the next token is an entity is by far the biggest error source, it will lead to relevant error propagation in real-world applications. Therefore and because the F1 score is best for SetLM we suggest that it is best handled implicitly. We note that with left-side context only, the decision if the next token belongs to an entity mention is extremely hard for a LM.

We suggest that mention length prediction is not crucial for a well-performing model. All systems tend to create shorter mentions than in the gold predictions to a similar extent and the EntityNLM re-implementation did not perform notably better than the other models without length prediction.

A main challenge in the models is the difficulty to find a good training setting. Unsatisfactorily, our models did not profit from more hidden units without pre-training, while a high number of hidden units was the modification that lead to the greatest performance boost for the baseline RNN-LM. We find it promising that with 64 hidden units, the Yang et al. re-implementation performs better than the RNN-LM, but this effect does not scale to larger hidden sizes.

7 Conclusion

Our evaluation of three LMs that explicitly model coreference decisions in comparison to standard RNN-LMs suggests that these procedures do not improve a LM in a general language modelling task in perplexity.

The overall performance and the entity prediction results suggest that the decision if the next token is an entity should be handled with a probability distribution over the set of entities rather than with the current hidden state alone.

We see a need for evaluations on larger high-quality annotated data sets to study if they can possibly improve the prediction process with left context only, and for evaluations on other genres. Short texts that are mostly news texts are probably not the genre that takes most profit of explicit entity information. It is possible that in longer texts or texts with complexly interacting characters that develop in the text, a language model would take greater profit from explicit entity modeling.

Despite the limitations of the current models, we regard it as worthwhile to invest in improvements, especially in the development of models that are less prone to error propagation, and to explore these models' potential.

Acknowledgements

This work was supported by the Swedish Research Council under grant 2017-930. We thank all anonymous reviewers for their constructive comments.

References

Dzmitry Bahdanau, Kyunghyun Cho, and Yoshua Bengio. 2014. Neural machine translation by jointly learning to align and translate. *arXiv preprint arXiv:1409.0473*.

Elizabeth Clark, Yangfeng Ji, and Noah A Smith. 2018. Neural text generation in stories using entity representations as context. In *Proceedings of the 2018 Conference of the North American Chapter of the Association for Computational Linguistics: Human Language Technologies, Volume 1 (Long Papers)*, pages 2250–2260.

Sepp Hochreiter and Jürgen Schmidhuber. 1997. Long short-term memory. *Neural Computation*, 9(8):1735–1780.

Yangfeng Ji, Chenhao Tan, Sebastian Martschat, Yejin Choi, and Noah A Smith. 2017. Dynamic entity representations in neural language models. *arXiv preprint arXiv:1708.00781*.

Diederik P Kingma and Jimmy Ba. 2014. Adam: A method for stochastic optimization. *arXiv preprint arXiv:1412.6980*.

Tomas Mikolov, Kai Chen, Greg Corrado, and Jeffrey Dean. 2013. Efficient estimation of word representations in vector space. *arXiv preprint arXiv:1301.3781*.

Vincent Ng. 2017. Machine learning for entity coreference resolution: A retrospective look at two decades of research. In *AAAI*, pages 4877–4884.

Adam Paszke, Sam Gross, Soumith Chintala, Gregory Chanan, Edward Yang, Zachary DeVito, Zeming Lin, Alban Desmaison, Luca Antiga, and Adam Lerer. 2017. Automatic differentiation in PyTorch.

Jeffrey Pennington, Richard Socher, and Christopher Manning. 2014. Glove: Global vectors for word representation. In *Proceedings of the 2014 Conference on Empirical Methods in Natural Language Processing (EMNLP)*, pages 1532–1543.

Nitish Srivastava, Geoffrey Hinton, Alex Krizhevsky, Ilya Sutskever, and Ruslan Salakhutdinov. 2014. Dropout: a simple way to prevent neural networks from overfitting. *The Journal of Machine Learning Research*, 15(1):1929–1958.

Martin Sundermeyer, Ralf Schlüter, and Hermann Ney. 2012. LSTM neural networks for language modeling. In *Thirteenth Annual Conference of the International Speech Communication Association*.

Ralph Weischedel, Martha Palmer, Mitchell Marcus, Eduard Hovy, Sameer Pradhan, Lance Ramshaw, Nianwen Xue, Ann Taylor, Jeff Kaufman, Michelle Franchini, et al. 2013. OntoNotes release 5.0 ldc2013t19. *Linguistic Data Consortium, Philadelphia, PA*.

Zichao Yang, Phil Blunsom, Chris Dyer, and Wang Ling. 2016. Reference-aware language models. *arXiv preprint arXiv:1611.01628*.

Jie Zhao, Yu Su, Ziyu Guan, and Huan Sun. 2017. An end-to-end deep framework for answer triggering with a novel group-level objective. In *Proceedings of the 2017 Conference on Empirical Methods in Natural Language Processing*, pages 1276–1282.

Cross-lingual NIL Entity Clustering for Low-resource Languages

Kevin Blissett and **Heng Ji**
Computer Science Department
Rensselaer Polytechnic Institute
{blissk,jih}@rpi.edu

Abstract

Clustering unlinkable entity mentions across documents in multiple languages (*cross-lingual NIL Clustering*) is an important task as part of Entity Discovery and Linking (EDL). This task has been largely neglected by the EDL community because it is challenging to outperform simple edit distance or other heuristics based baselines. We propose a novel approach based on encoding the orthographic similarity of the mentions using a Recurrent Neural Network (RNN) architecture. Our model adapts a training procedure from the one-shot facial recognition literature in order to achieve this. We also perform several exploratory probing tasks on our name encodings in order to determine what specific types of information are likely to be encoded by our model. Experiments show our approach provides up to a 6.6% absolute CEAFm F-Score improvement over state-of-the-art methods and successfully captures phonological relations across languages.

1 Introduction

The objective of Entity Discovery and Linking (EDL; Ji et al. 2014) is to identify within a text or set of texts all of the names which refer to entities in the world and then link those name mentions to a Knowledge Base (KB). Common approaches to EDL, however, often ignore the question of what to do with name mentions that cannot be linked to the KB.

Clustering unlinkable mentions is often critical to successfully extracting relevant information from a given corpus about emergent situations. For example, before June of 2013, no Wikipedia entry existed for Edward Snowden. But, suddenly, in that month, properly identifying and clustering thousands of mentions in dozens of languages for this entity became a key task for IE systems focused on breaking news. Similar situations occur when significant political events occur in remote areas. For example, in November of 2015, protests broke out in the town of Ginci in Ethiopia (Pinaud and Raleigh, 2017), but Ginci also does not appear in Wikipedia.

Orthographic similarity provides one of the best single indicators of which mentions ought to be clustered. By relying on this clue, given two parallel sentences, human annotators are often able to accurately determine which names refer to the same entity even without speaking the relevant languages (Lin et al., 2018). However, this remarkable ability cannot be captured using simple string similarity measures (such as edit distance) alone. For example, Figure 1 shows the edit distance between several mentions of the same entity *Ethiopia* as they appeared in an Oromo corpus. The edit distances between various mentions vary widely, making it extremely difficult to design a clustering system based only on this metric and a predefined threshold.

	#ethiopa	ethiipiyaafi	ethiophiyaattuu	ethiopia	itiyophiyaa	itoophiyaawwidha
#ethiopa	0	7	9	2	8	13
ethiipiyaafi		0	6	5	7	10
ethiophiyaattuu			0	7	7	9
ethiopia				0	6	11
itiyophiyaa					0	8
itoophiyaawwidha						0

Figure 1: Edit distance between several mentions of the same entity *Ethiopia* from an LDC Oromo news corpus.

We propose to encode name mentions using a character-based Recurrent Neural Network (RNN). We train this model in a manner inspired by work on the analogous task of one-shot facial

Proceedings of the 2nd Workshop on Computational Models of Reference, Anaphora and Coreference (CRAC 2019), pages 20–25,
Minneapolis, USA, June 7, 2019.

recognition as addressed by (Schroff et al., 2015). In that task, a single model encodes images into a shared space. Images of the same person are identified by measuring which encoding vectors are near one another in that space. Analogously, we consider different name mentions of the same entity as different "views" of that entity. Mentions are encoded such that mentions likely to refer to the same entity are close to one another in the encoding space. Mentions can then be clustered using standard clustering techniques.

2 Approach

2.1 Basic Model

In our approach, input mentions are represented as a sequence of vectors $\boldsymbol{X} = \{\boldsymbol{x}_1, \boldsymbol{x}_2, ..., \boldsymbol{x}_L\}$ where $\boldsymbol{x}_i$ is a vector representing the i-th character of a mention and L is the number of characters in the mention. $\boldsymbol{x}_i$ is an embedding vector for each character trained jointly with the rest of the model. Input sequences are then fed to a bidirectional RNN based on Gated Recurrent Units (GRU; Cho et al. 2014). The hidden representations $\boldsymbol{h}_i$ produced by the model are passed to a fully-connected layer which creates an unnormalized encoding for the mention $\boldsymbol{n}_i$ which is normalized to unit length to produce the final encoding for the mention $\boldsymbol{y}_i$. A margin α, is set during training, which controls the target minimum distance between any mention x and any other mention which does not refer to the same entity.

Mentions are clustered into disjoint subsets S_i using the DBSCAN algorithm. We select DBSCAN primarily because it does not require the user to pre-specify the number of expected clusters. We set the hyperparameter ϵ for the clustering by performing a grid search over possible values and selecting the value that maximizes the CEAFm score (Ji et al., 2014) on the training data.

Typical hyperparameter values for the encoding model are summarized in Table 2. Dropout was also used in order to provide regularization when training data was limited.

2.2 Training Procedure

During training, the model is presented with triplets of name mentions (x_a, x_p, x_n). These triplets consist of an *anchor* x_a, a *positive* x_p and a *negative* x_n. The anchor is drawn from the set of name mentions M_A which have at least two name mentions in their cluster. That is, given the vocabulary of all name mentions V

$$\begin{aligned} M_A = \{x_a | (\exists x)[x_a \in V \wedge \texttt{refers\_to}(x_a, e) \\ \wedge \texttt{refers\_to}(x, e) \\ \wedge x_a \neq x]\} \end{aligned}$$

The positive is a name mention drawn from the set of name mentions M_{Pi} which refer to same entity as the i-th anchor mention x_{ai}.

$$\begin{aligned} M_{Pi} = \{x_p | x_p \in V \wedge \texttt{refers\_to}(x_p, e) \\ \wedge \texttt{refers\_to}(x_{ai}, e) \\ \wedge x_p \neq x_{ai}\} \end{aligned}$$

An example anchor-positive pair may consist of the names *(Bill Gates, Gates)*. The negative is a name that does not refer to the same entity as the anchor. Rather than selecting the negative randomly, we select the negative example which has an encoding closest to the anchor as measured by Euclidean distance. In this way, we follow the example of (Schroff et al., 2015) and select for the negative a name calculated to provide useful information about areas of poor model performance. For example, the anchor-positive-negative triplet *(Bill Gates, Gates, Gaines)* is more difficult and therefore likely to be informative to the model than the triplet *(Bill Gates, Gates, Smith)*. Over the course of training, this negative sampling technique ensures that the model is consistently exposed to informative examples. Randomly sampling the negative provides no guarantee that the model will ever see the triplets it most needs to improve. Our experimental results show that this non-random negative sampling led to a meaningful improvement in model performance.

More specifically, negatives are sampled according to the following procedure: before training and after the model is presented with each training batch, all names in the dataset are encoded by the model in its current state and the encodings are cached. For any given pair of an anchor encoding and a positive encoding (x_a, x_p), a name is chosen from the dataset vocabulary of name mentions V to serve as the negative x_n such that the encoding of the negative is as close to the anchor encoding as possible. Treating our encoding model as a single function f, we select the negative according to the following equation:

$$\underset{x_n \epsilon V}{\arg\min} \|f(x_a) - f(x_n)\|_2^2$$

	Naive Baseline	**Edit Distance**	**Random Sampling**	**Our Approach**
Oromo	0.531	0.840	0.827	**0.868**
Tigrinya	0.573	0.806	0.828	**0.872**
Oromo + Tigrinya	0.454	0.828	0.817	**0.841**

Table 1: CEAFm F-score for baseline models compared to system performance.

Hidden Dim.	64
Num. RNN Layers	2
Embedding Dim.	16
Margin α	0.2
Output Dim.	16

Table 2: Typical hyperparameters for the encoding model.

As an optimization, in practice we subject the negative to the following additional constraint:

$$\|f(x_a) - f(x_n)\|_2^2 > \|f(x_a) - f(x_p)\|_2^2$$

This produces what is referred to as a "semi-hard" example in (Schroff et al., 2015), and was found to be an important optimization to ensure that the model converges.

Triplets constructed according to this procedure are then encoded by the model and the model is trained to optimize the following loss function:

$$\sum_i^N \left[\|f(x_i^a) - f(x_i^p)\|_2^2 - \|f(x_i^a) - f(x_i^n)\|_2^2 + \alpha \right]_+$$

A single epoch of training consists of showing the model all triplets composed of every possible anchor-positive pair and their corresponding negative x_i^n.

Our method can be applied to cross-lingual datasets without modification. New anchor-positive pairs are constructed by pairing mentions that refer to the same entity regardless of the language of origin and training proceeds as normal.

3 Experiment

3.1 Data and Scoring Metric

We use two languages, Oromo and Tigrinya, for our experiments. Both languages are members of the Afro-Asiatic language family, but they belong to separate branches of that family and have distinct phonologies, grammars, and writing systems from one another. We select these languages as exemplars of extremely low-resource languages. These languages have been used in the standard NIST shared tasks LoreHLT[1]. Specifically we use data from the DARPA LORELEI program[2] because these data sets include human annotated ground truth. Each mention in the dataset belongs to one of the four following types: person, organization, geopolitical entity, or location. We also create a combined Oromo-Tigrinya dataset by merging the two datasets. Table 3 shows the detailed data statistics. The test set consists only of NIL mentions. We produce it by collecting all NIL mentions from the complete dataset and dividing them randomly. One portion is used as the test set and the other is used during model training as a development set. All non-NIL mentions are also used during training. Our final model for Oromo is trained on 4101 mentions from 327 clusters while for Tigrinya we use 3990 mentions from 330 clusters.

	Tigrinya	**Oromo**
Test Set NIL Mentions	640	894
Test Set NIL Clusters	78	70

Table 3: Statistics for experimental datasets. *Test Set NIL Clusters* refers to the number of clusters with size > 1.

3.2 Results

We compare our system's score to three baselines. The first is a naive baseline which gives the score on the dataset if every mention is assigned a unique cluster ID. We also compare the scores to a baseline based primarily on edit distance and enhanced with simple heuristics (such as merging a mention of a person's last name with mentions of their full name that appear in the same document). The edit distance baseline does not incorporate any special weighting for edits, but does use the Python Unidecode package (Solc, 2009) in order to map Tigrinya into ascii characters in the combined dataset task. Finally, we report the

[1]https://www.nist.gov/itl/iad/mig/lorehlt-evaluations

[2]LDC2017E57 and LDC2017E58 in the LDC Catalog

results for a model that is the same as our final model, but trained by sampling the negative randomly. Table 1 shows the results.

Our model improves on the baseline for all datasets. Of special note is the increase in performance we get from using the negative sampling technique designed by (Schroff et al., 2015). For all datasets, sampling the most difficult negative rather than sampling randomly gives a significant increase in performance of about 4% CEAFm F-score. In our experience, this technique also seemed to help reduce overfitting by varying the training data from batch to batch.

The baseline model performed significantly worse on Tigrinya compared to Oromo. The reasons for this are not entirely clear, but it could be due to the fact that the Ge'ez script used for Tigrinya is an abugida (a writing system which represents entire syllables with single characters) and contains a large number of characters. This means that syllables (and by extension, words) that are phonetically similar are spelled with entirely different characters even if they share some vowel or consonant sounds. Notably, applying the Unidecode package did not seem to remedy this issue. Whatever the problem, our model did not seem to encounter the same struggles and actually performed better on Tigrinya relative to the other tasks.

4 Probing Mention Encodings

In order to illustrate some of the linguistic information captured by our model, we give an example examination of the vectors produced by several closely related input sequences. This qualitative analysis illustrates that our model learns which letter alternations are most and least important when transliterating words between given language pairs.

We hypothesize that alternating among characters that represent very similar sounds between two languages should make little difference in the final encoding. By determining which alternations cause the smallest difference in output encodings, we can ascertain which letters the model finds are most interchangeable for this language pair.

We train an encoder model on the Google Arabic to English transliteration dataset (Rosca and Breuel, 2016), for this example.

Table 4 shows the result of alternating the first letter of the name 'peter' after training our model.

Replacement	Distance
p → b	0.026
p → baa	0.060
p → shiin	1.05
p → raa	1.02

Table 4: First letter replacements for the name 'peter' which make the largest and smallest differences in the output encoding.

Shown in the right column is the distance of the output encoding from the original encoding after making each replacement. Our model encodes names beginning with 'p', 'b', or the Arabic 'baa' similarly because alternations among these sounds do not often distinguish the names of entities from one another in this language pair. This is because Arabic has no equivalent of the English 'p' sound, and thus, in English names containing 'p's and 'b's, those letters are most commonly transliterated to the single Arabic character 'baa'.

5 Related Work

The task of clustering NIL entity mentions was introduced in the TAC2014 Knowledge Base Population track (Ji et al., 2014). Approaches to this task have included using direct string or substring matches (Cassidy et al., 2011; Jiang et al., 2017) and edit distance based metrics (Ploch et al., 2011; Greenfield et al., 2016). Elaborations on these methods include leveraging systems for entity coreference (Huynh et al., 2013), query expansion (Radford et al., 2011; Yu et al., 2013) using context features either on the document level (Fahrni et al., 2013; Graus et al., 2012; Hong et al., 2014) or the sentence level (Ploch et al., 2011), and applying hand-crafted heuristic rules (Al-Badrashiny et al., 2017; Li et al., 2016). Our method differs from the above by clustering based on a measurement of surface similarities between words, but not relying directly on edit distance.

We found in our experiments that the standard DBSCAN algorithm for clustering (Ester et al., 1996) performed well, but many additional clustering techniques for NIL entities were explored in (Tamang et al., 2012). In particular, hierarchical agglomerative clustering methods have seen some success (Zhang et al., 2012; Graus et al., 2012; Ploch et al., 2012) Because our work focused on the effective encoding of word forms rather than new techniques for clustering the encoded vectors, we did not pursue these techniques.

Neural machine transliteration models have used RNNs to encode input character sequences into fixed length vectors (Finch et al., 2016; Jadidinejad, 2016; Ameur et al., 2017). This is similar to our own approach, but where these models produce vectors only as an intermediate step (to be later fed to a decoder network), we use the vectors produced by the encoder directly and do not use a decoder at all.

Our training procedure relies on a negative sampling technique from the one-shot facial recognition literature (Schroff et al., 2015). More specifically, we sample our negative samples according to the method used to train FaceNet.

6 Conclusion and Future Work

We construct a model to encode the surface features of words and cluster those encodings to determine which unlinkable mentions refer to the same entities. Our model shows improvement over baseline models based on edit distance and ad hoc heuristic rules. Future work may include incorporating more information from the context surrounding the name mentions and exploration of new encoding architectures and clustering algorithms.

Acknowledgments

This research is based upon work supported in part by U.S. DARPA LORELEI Program # HR0011-15-C-0115, and the Office of the Director of National Intelligence (ODNI), Intelligence Advanced Research Projects Activity (IARPA), via contract # FA8650-17-C-9116, and ARL NS-CTA No. W911NF-09-2-0053. The views and conclusions contained herein are those of the authors and should not be interpreted as necessarily representing the official policies, either expressed or implied, of DARPA, ODNI, IARPA, or the U.S. Government. The U.S. Government is authorized to reproduce and distribute reprints for governmental purposes notwithstanding any copyright annotation therein.

References

Mohamed Al-Badrashiny, Jason Bolton, Arun Tejasvi Chaganty, Kevin Clark, Craig Harman, Lifu Huang, Matthew Lamm, Jinhao Lei, Di Lu, Xiaoman Pan, et al. 2017. Tinkerbell: Cross-lingual cold-start knowledge base construction. In *TAC*, pages 1–12.

Mohamed Seghir Hadj Ameur, Farid Meziane, and Ahmed Guessoum. 2017. Arabic machine transliteration using an attention-based encoder-decoder model. *Procedia Computer Science*, 117:287–297.

Taylor Cassidy, Zheng Chen, Javier Artiles, Heng Ji, Hongbo Deng, Lev-Arie Ratinov, Jing Zheng, Jiawei Han, and Dan Roth. 2011. CUNY-UIUC-SRI TAC-KBP2011 entity linking system description. In *TAC*, pages 1–13.

Kyunghyun Cho, Bart van Merrienboer, Caglar Gulcehre, Dzmitry Bahdanau, Fethi Bougares, Holger Schwenk, and Yoshua Bengio. 2014. Learning phrase representations using RNN encoder–decoder for statistical machine translation. In *EMNLP*, pages 1724–1734.

Martin Ester, Hans-Peter Kriegel, Jörg Sander, and Xiaowei Xu. 1996. A density-based algorithm for discovering clusters in large spatial databases with noise. In *KDD*, pages 226–231. AAAI Press.

Angela Fahrni, Benjamin Heinzerling, Thierry Göckel, and Michael Strube. 2013. HITS' monolingual and cross-lingual entity linking system at TAC 2013. In *TAC*, pages 1–10.

Andrew Finch, Lemao Liu, Xiaolin Wang, and Eiichiro Sumita. 2016. Target-bidirectional neural models for machine transliteration. In *Proceedings of the Sixth Named Entity Workshop*, pages 78–82.

David Graus, Tom Kenter, Marc Bron, Edgar Meij, Maarten De Rijke, et al. 2012. Context-based entity linking-University of Amsterdam at TAC 2012. In *TAC*, pages 1–6.

Kara Greenfield, Rajmonda S Caceres, Michael Coury, Kelly Geyer, Youngjune Gwon, Jason Matterer, Alyssa Mensch, Cem Safak Sahin, and Olga Simek. 2016. A reverse approach to named entity extraction and linking in microposts. In *#Microposts*, pages 67–69.

Yu Hong, Xiaobin Wang, Yadong Chen, Jian Wang, Tongtao Zhang, Jin Zheng, Dian Yu, Qi Li, Boliang Zhang, Han Wang, et al. 2014. RPI-BLENDER TAC-KBP2014 knowledge base population system. In *TAC*, pages 1–12.

Huy M Huynh, Trong T Nguyen, and Tru H Cao. 2013. Using coreference and surrounding contexts for entity linking. In *RIVF*, pages 1–5. IEEE.

Amir H Jadidinejad. 2016. Neural machine transliteration: Preliminary results. *arXiv preprint arXiv:1609.04253*.

Heng Ji, Joel Nothman, and Ben Hachey. 2014. Overview of TAC-KBP2014 entity discovery and linking tasks. In *TAC*, pages 1–15.

Shanshan Jiang, Yihan Li, Tianyi Qin, Qian Meng, and Bin Dong. 2017. SRCB entity discovery and linking (EDL) and event nugget systems for TAC 2017. In *TAC*, pages 1–11.

Manling Li, Xinlei Chen, Yantao Jia, Yuanzhuo Wang, Xiaolong Jin, Zixuan Li, Juan Yao, Fan Yang, Yunqi Qiu, Jialin Su, et al. 2016. OpenKN at TAC KBP 2016. In *TAC*, pages 1–8.

Ying Lin, Cash Costello, Boliang Zhang, Di Lu, Heng Ji, James Mayfield, and Paul McNamee. 2018. Platforms for non-speakers annotating names in any language. In *Proceedings of ACL 2018, System Demonstrations*, pages 1–6.

Margaux Pinaud and Clionadh Raleigh. 2017. Data analysis: The roots of popular mobilization in Ethiopia.

Danuta Ploch, Leonhard Hennig, Ernesto William De Luca, and Sahin Albayrak. 2011. DAI approaches to the TAC-KBP 2011 entity linking task. In *TAC*, pages 1–9.

Danuta Ploch, Leonhard Hennig, Angelina Duka, Ernesto William De Luca, and Sahin Albayrak. 2012. GerNED: A German corpus for named entity disambiguation. In *LREC*, pages 3886–3893.

Will Radford, Ben Hachey, Matthew Honnibal, Joel Nothman, and James R Curran. 2011. Naïve but effective NIL clustering baselines–CMCRC at TAC 2011. In *TAC*, pages 1–3.

Mihaela Rosca and Thomas Breuel. 2016. Sequence-to-sequence neural network models for transliteration. *arXiv preprint arXiv:1610.09565*.

Florian Schroff, Dmitry Kalenichenko, and James Philbin. 2015. FaceNet: A unified embedding for face recognition and clustering. In *Proceedings of the IEEE conference on computer vision and pattern recognition*, pages 815–823.

Tomaz Solc. 2009. Unidecode. [Online; accessed 10 December 2018].

Suzanne Tamang, Zheng Chen, and Heng Ji. 2012. CUNY BLENDER TAC-KBP2012 entity linking system and slot filling validation system. In *TAC*, pages 1–21.

Dian Yu, Haibo Li, Taylor Cassidy, Qi Li, Hongzhao Huang, Zheng Chen, Heng Ji, Yongzhong Zhang, and Dan Roth. 2013. RPI-BLENDER TAC-KBP2013 knowledge base population system. In *TAC*, pages 1–14.

Tao Zhang, Kang Liu, and Jun Zhao. 2012. The NL-PRIR entity linking system at TAC 2012. In *TAC*, pages 1–5.

Cross-lingual Incongruences in the Annotation of Coreference

Ekaterina Lapshinova-Koltunski[1] **Sharid Loáiciga**[2]
Christian Hardmeier[3] **Pauline Krielke**[1]
[1]Department of Language Science and Technology, Saarland University, Germany
[2]CLASP, University of Gothenburg, Sweden
[3]Department of Linguistics and Philology, Uppsala University, Sweden
e.lapshinova@mx.uni-saarland.de sharid.loaiciga@gu.se
christian.hardmeier@lingfil.uu.se
pauline.krielke@uni-saarland.de

Abstract

In the present paper, we deal with incongruences in English-German multilingual coreference annotation and present automated methods to discover them. More specifically, we automatically detect full coreference chains in parallel texts and analyse discrepancies in their annotations. In doing so, we wish to find out whether the discrepancies rather derive from language typological constraints, from the translation or the actual annotation process. The results of our study contribute to the referential analysis of similarities and differences across languages and support evaluation of cross-lingual coreference annotation. They are also useful for cross-lingual coreference resolution systems and contrastive linguistic studies.

1 Introduction

Linguistically annotated parallel corpora in multiple languages are valuable resources for language technology, linguistic research and translation studies. To be maximally useful for such applications, the annotation should accurately reflect linguistically relevant contrasts across the languages. Ideally, parallel structures should be annotated identically in all languages, and any differences in the annotated structures should indicate either language contrasts or non-trivial effects of the translation process. Unfortunately, experience shows that this is very difficult to achieve in practice. Annotated resources with texts in multiple languages invariably exhibit cross-linguistic variation that arises spuriously as a result of the annotation process and does not reflect any linguistically relevant phenomena.

We refer to the differences in annotated parallel texts as annotation *incongruences*. Manual detection of incongruences is not only time- and effort-consuming, but also inefficient. Despite the ubiquity of this problem in all kind of parallel linguistic annotation, it has received little attention in the existing works.

In this paper, we address the problem of cross-lingual incongruences in the manual annotation of coreference. To our knowledge, none of the existing studies on parallel coreference annotation (Dipper and Zinsmeister, 2012; Zikánová et al., 2015; Grishina and Stede, 2017) addresses this issue. We analyse the incongruences in coreference chains in a subset of the corpus ParCorFull (Lapshinova-Koltunski et al., 2018), an English-German parallel corpus containing manual annotations of coreference.

We automatically extract annotated chains from the corpus, create an alignment between chains in the source and target language and identify those that do not have parallel equivalents in the source or the target language. Among the parallel chains, we detect those with differences in English and German. Our use of word alignments to map coreference structures between language is similar to the existing studies on annotation projection (e.g. Yarowsky et al., 2001) or specifically on multilingual coreference projection (Postolache et al., 2006; Ogrodniczuk, 2013; Grishina and Stede, 2015; Novák, 2018). However, in contrast to annotation projection, we do not aim to produce any automatic annotations. Instead, we use automated methods to discover incongruences in the existing annotations produced manually on parallel texts.

The cross-lingual variation in the chains is then analysed both quantitatively and qualitatively. We develop a typology of the incongruences encountered in ParCorFull, illustrated with corpus examples, and present empirical results on the prevalence of different types of variations using a corpus sample.

The results of this study facilitate the analysis of similarities and idiosyncracies in coreference

Proceedings of the 2nd Workshop on Computational Models of Reference, Anaphora and Coreference (CRAC 2019), pages 26–34,
Minneapolis, USA, June 7, 2019.

across languages and support the evaluation of cross-lingual coreference annotation. In this way, they contribute to contrastive linguistic and translation studies as well as to cross-lingual coreference resolution. Moreover, the method applied in this work can be used for automatic evaluation of other manually annotated structures in parallel data.

2 Annotation Incongruences

2.1 Definition of Incongruences

Annotation of multilingual data requires definition of universal categories that exist in all the languages involved. For instance, the English chain in example (1) is represented by a nominal phrase, a relative and a personal pronoun (*a close friend – who – she*). The corresponding German translation contains the three-member chain that also consists of a nominal phrase, a relative and a personal pronoun (*eine enge Freundin – die – ihr*).

(1) a. *I had [a close friend] from college [who]'d gone through a divorce and wanted to have children. And so [she] and I have a daughter, and mother and daughter live in Texas.*

b. *Ich hatte [eine enge Freundin] aus Uni-Tagen, [die] eine Scheidung hinter sich hatte und Kinder wollte. Mit [ihr] habe ich also eine Tochter, und Mutter und Tochter leben in Texas .*

This is an ideal case of a parallel coreference chain, the only difference being the case of the personal pronoun *she/ihr*. However, even typologically close languages, like English and German, have systemic differences in the range of linguistic means triggering coreference (Kunz and Lapshinova-Koltunski, 2015; Novák and Nedoluzhko, 2015; Kunz and Steiner, 2012; Kunz, 2010). Moreover, translated texts differ from non-translated ones in terms of language use, as shown by corpus-based studies on translationese (Baroni and Bernardini, 2006; Ilisei et al., 2010, among others). As a result, parallel texts do not always contain identical chains. Equivalent chains may differ in the types of referring expressions[1] or they may differ in the number of referring expressions. Besides that, translations may contain chains that are not present in the source texts, and source texts may contain chains that do not appear in the target. We refer to these language-typology and translation-process-driven differences in the parallel chains as *annotation incongruences*. Furthermore, we realise that the differences in the annotated structures may also have their origin in the process of manual annotation, i.e. human annotators may have interpreted the source and the target text in a different way (especially if the annotation of the source and the target texts was performed independently), or may simply have made errors.

[1]Note that the differences in the types of referring expressions within the parallel chains are beyond the scope of this study.

2.2 Typology of incongruences

We suggest that we can classify incongruences into four groups according to their sources: 1. explicitation; 2. implicitation; 3. annotation interpretation and 4. annotation error. The first two groups (1 and 2) are related to the hypothesis of explicitation, while the latter two groups (3 and 4) are related to the annotation process rather than the translation process.

1. Explicitation The hypothesis of explicitation was formulated by Blum-Kulka (1986). We adopt the definition of explicitation (and implicitation) introduced by Klaudy and Karoly (2005, p. 15), according to which explicitation takes place when a translation contains more specific linguistic units (instead of more general units in the source), or new linguistic units (not present in the source), a phrase is extended to clause level, a sentence is split into two sentences, etc. For the explanation of explicitation-induced incongruences, we use Klaudy's notion of operational asymmetry and her classification of explicitation into obligatory, optional, pragmatic and translation-inherent (see Klaudy, 2008, 106–107). Obligatory explicitation is dictated by differences in the syntactic and semantic structure of languages. Optional explicitation is related to the differences in text-building strategies and stylistic preferences. In the case of pragmatic explicitation, there is implicit cultural information and translators often need to include explanations. In example (2), the English source does not contain any coreference chains, whereas its German translation does. The German coreference chain includes two members: a noun phrase and a relative pronoun introducing a relative clause. The information contained in this relative clause was packed into a participle construction (non-finite *ing*-construction) in the English source. This clause type has a direct equivalent in German, the present participle *schreibend* ("writing"). However, the English *ing*-form is used much more widely than the German present. In particular, participial clauses are restricted to formal written registers in German and can sound stilted and they are used much less frequently than clauses with *ing*-forms in English (Durrell, 2011, p.281–285). This is a case of an obligatory explicitation – a translator has to add a relative clause and thus, a pronoun, to express the information, as the language system requires one. Further cases include an addition of a reflexive pronoun required by the verb valency.

(2) a. *It turned out that tens of thousands of autonomous individuals writing an encyclopedia...*
b. *Es stellte sich heraus, dass [Zehntausende von autonomen Einzelpersonen], [die] ein Lexikon schreiben...*

The decision to use more explicit constructions can have stylistic reasons, as in example (3). Here, the English source has a coordinated verb phrase which does not require a subject for the second verb, and the source chain has two members only. Instead, we find two subordinate clauses in the German target (corresponding to the two verbal clauses in English) which require another mention of the subject, and thus, a chain of three members.

(3) a. *...business strategy has always been premised on [assumptions about technology], that [those assumptions] are changing, and, in fact, changing quite dramatically...*
b. *...dass Geschäftsstrategie immer schon auf [Annahmen über Technologie] basiert, dass sich [diese Annahmen] ändern, und dass [sie] sich sogar ziemlich dramatisch ändern....*

Other explicitation cases are translation-inherent as they depend on a translator's decision, as in example (4). The German chain has the element *ihre* ("their"). This is a possessive pronoun modifying the noun phrase *ihre Kinder*, which is, however, a part of another coreference chain. In the source, this information is expressed via the pronoun *them*, where no modifying element is necessary.

(4) a. *And I suddenly thought, most deaf children are born to [hearing parents]. [Those hearing parents] tend to try to cure them.*
b. *Und da dachte ich plötzlich, dass die meisten tauben Kinder [hörende Eltern] haben, und [diese] in der Regel versuchen, [ihre] Kinder zu heilen.*

While obligatory (language-typology-driven) explicitation is easy to identify, it is difficult to differentiate between optional, pragmatic and translation-inherent cases that are translation-process-driven. For this reason, we classify the analysed cases exposing explicitation into two groups only: obligatory and non-obligatory.

2. Implicitation Implicitation is an opposite process to explicitation and means that translations can be shorter, more compressed; e.g., the subject (which was a member of a chain in the source) was omitted and a coordinated verb phrase was used instead. In other cases, the information is packed into a different, more compact construction without a mention. As well as explicitation, implicitation can be obligatory and non-obligatory (see Klaudy and Károly, 2005, p. 16–17). In example (5), the English source contains a chain of three members and the third mention (*that*) is not present in the corresponding German sentence. This German sentence contains the discourse element *hier* which links this to the previous context. However, this element is not a member of the coreference chain, as the relation and its scope is different. The element *hier* refers to the whole situation and not to *logic*.

(5) a. *...and it maps exactly on to [the kind of Porter-Henderson logic] [that] we've been talking about. And [that] is, about data.*
b. *und es ordnet sich genau in [die Art der Porter-Henderson-Logik] ein, über [die] wir gesprochen haben. Es geht [hier] um Daten .*

Implicitation cases can also be related to the specific genre of our data – TED talks are subtitled and not translated, and compressing information is a core strategy in subtitling. This is a frequent cause of optional, non-obligatory implicitation. The kind of compression we observe in our translations results from the guidelines of reducing information to tackle reading-speed issues[2]. In the

[2]See the guidelines under `https://translations.ted.com/How_to_Compress_Subtitles`

German sentence in (6), we observe a compression of the information contained in the English source: *weekend I spent with them* vs. *gemeinsames Wochenende* ("joint weekend/weekend together").

(6) a. *And the first weekend I spent with [them] – the first of many – I recorded more than 20 hours of conversation.*

b. *Am ersten gemeinsamen Wochenende – einem von vielen – zeichnete ich mehr als 20 Stunden an Gesprächsstoff auf.*

3. Different interpretations Annotators sometimes interpret German texts differently from the English sources. This is especially frequent with ambiguous cases, when it is difficult to understand exactly which components participate in the coreference relation. In example (7), the English texts contains two chains (*when we collect... – This – it – this* and *a revolution in medicine – this*). In the German translation, there is only one non-entity chain *wenn wir... – dies – es – darüber*. A different interpretation in the translation results from the fact that the English sentence contains the full verb *drive* with *a revolution in medicine* as a direct object. This creates a different identity and thus, a different coreference chain. In the German translation, the nominal phrase *eine Revolution in der Medizin* is linked to *es* with a copula verb and is, therefore, a part of the same identity expressed via pronoun.

(7) a. *Think what happens [when we collect all of that data and we can put it together in order to find patterns we wouldn't see before]$_1$. [This]$_1$, I would suggest, perhaps [it]$_1$ will take a while, but [this]$_1$ will drive [a revolution in medicine]$_2$. Fabulous, lots of people talk about [this]$_2$.*

b. *Was passiert, [wenn wir all diese Daten sammeln und wir sie zusammenfügen können, um Muster zu erkennen, die wir nicht vorher sehen konnten]$_1$. Vielleicht dauert [dies]$_1$ ja noch eine Weile, aber [es]$_1$ wird eine Revolution in der Medizin. Fabelhaft – sehr viele Leute sprechen [darüber]$_1$.*

4. Annotation error This type of incongruences emerges due to errors in the manual annotation, such as if mentions were not included into the chains they should have been included to or there were two shorter chains annotated instead of one longer one.

3 Data

For our analysis, we use a subset of the parallel corpus ParCorFull (Lapshinova-Koltunski et al., 2018). This corpus contains English texts and their German translations that were annotated with coreference chains. The underlying coreference scheme was designed for uniform coreference annotations of a multilingual corpus (see Lapshinova-Koltunski and Hardmeier, 2017, for details).

The annotated elements (markables) in this corpus include pronouns, nouns, nominal phrases or elliptical constructions that are parts of a coreference pair (antecedent-anaphora), as well as verb phrases or clauses being antecedents of event anaphora. The annotated antecedents are of two different types: entities and events. For the analysis in this paper, we restrict ourselves to chains with nominal antecedents, excluding event reference with verbal and clausal antecedents.

Entities can be represented by a pronoun or a noun phrase. Antecedents can be split, i.e. two pronouns or two nouns (disjoint in a text) constitute one antecedent – all components of the antecedent are linked to a referring expression. The annotated referring expressions (anaphors) are represented by pronouns (personal, demonstrative, relative and reflexive) and nominal phrases. Demonstrative pronouns may also refer to locations (*there, here*) and time (*then, now*). There are also pronominal adverbs formed by replacing a preposition and a pronoun, like *für+das* → *dafür* ("for this"). These are very common in German, but sound rather archaic and are generally avoided in English. Coreferring nominal phrases include proper names, nominal premodifiers, full nominal phrases and nominal phrases with quantifiers (see more details in Lapshinova-Koltunski et al., 2018). Linguistic chains may also include substitution and ellipsis in addition to referring expressions[3] – they often occur in similar contexts as coreference if considered cross-lingually.

The whole version of ParCorFull contains ca. 161,000 words. Our subset includes 77,216 word of TED talks (39,764 of the English TED talks and

[3]Although substitution and ellipsis do not express identity, they are included into the annotation scheme of ParCorFull, as they express the relations of near-identity and may occur in the same context as coreference.

37,452 of their German translations) and 21,237 words of news (10,644 English and 10,593 German texts).

4 Extraction Method

As mentioned in Section 3, we concentrate on the extraction of entity coreference chains only. We start by computing word level alignments between the source and target sides of the corpus in both directions using Giza++ (Och and Ney, 2003) with grow-diag-final symmetrization (Koehn et al., 2005). To align chains, we compute a matching score between each pair of source and target chains in the document, based on the alignment points they share. Alignment points are words in the source language aligned to words in the target language. Since word alignments are not necessarily one to one, each word may have no, one or multiple alignment points (Koehn, 2010).

For each potential chain pair, we take all the words in the source chain (all mentions) and count their alignment points with the words in the target chain, and repeat the process in the other direction. We then compute the average between the alignment points source-target and target-source and take the pair with the highest score as a pair match:

$$C_1 = |\{s \in S | \exists t \in T : (s,t) \in A\}|$$
$$C_2 = |\{t \in T | \exists s \in S : (s,t) \in A\}|$$
$$\text{score} = (C_1 + C_2)/2$$

where S and T are the sets of word indices belonging to the English and German chain, respectively, and A is the set of alignment points (pairs of source and target indices).

Potentially, two pairs of chains could have the same score. This never occurred with the relatively short nominal chains we considered for this paper. However, we expect it to happen with longer chains, for instance those corresponding to events.

5 Results

5.1 Automatic extraction

Our extraction procedure yields different categories of automatically identified incongruences. We group them according to the categories in Table 1.

I **Matching chains.** We approximate the concept of matching chains by considering pairs of chains in which both the source and the target chains contain the same number of mentions – as in example (1), where the English source chain *a close friend – who – she* corresponds to the German chain *eine enge Freundin – die – ihr.* While this simple operationalisation misses certain interesting transformation (such as alternations between pronouns and named entities, or changes in the order of the mentions), it allows us to concentrate on cases II and III, where changes are happening with certainty.

II **Overlapping chains.** Here we have matching chain pairs with a different number of mentions in either side of the corpus. We subdivide them according to the chain length with longer chain either in the English source, i.e., English has more mentions, or in the German translations, i.e., more German mentions.

III **Unpaired chains.** These are chains in either side of the corpus for which no chain correspondence is found. In the sample data under analysis, all cases of this type are German chains without a correspondence in English.

The results show that the analysed subcorpus contains approximately 32% chain matches, i.e., equivalent chains that have the same number of referring expression. These chains may still differ in the type of referring expressions contained in these chains. However, this variation is beyond the scope of this study. We restrict our analysis to the equivalent chains with a different number of mentions (overlapping chains) that constitute approximately 36% of the extracted chains. In this case, it is difficult to extract mention correspondences automatically. However, it can be seen that among the overlapping chains, most frequently, the German chains are longer than their English counterparts (334 vs. 210). Last, we also observe a considerable number of chains annotated in the German translation only (31%), whereas there are just a few cases of the unpaired English chains, i.e., those annotated in the source text only.

We assume that explicitation in our data is represented by cases where we observe more German mentions and unpaired German chains, whereas implicitation is related to the categories of more English mentions and unpaired English chains. Along these lines, explicitation would comprise

Chain category		TED #	TED %	News #	News %	Total #	Total %	Analysis
Matching	same number of mentions	392	32	84	33	476	32	
Overlapping	more English mentions	174	14	36	14	210	14	Implicitation
	more German mentions	293	24	41	16	334	22	Explicitation
Unpaired	English chains	0	0	9	4	9	1	Implicitation
	German chains	376	30	84	33	460	31	Explicitation
Total number of chains		1235	100	254	100	1489	100	

Table 1: Incongruences found automatically in the annotation of coreferential chains in the ParCorFull corpus.

Types of incongruences	TED #	TED %	News #	News %
Explicitation	40	37.4	27	41.5
Implicitation	7	6.5	8	12.3
Dif. interpetation	16	15.0	0	00.0
Annontation error	44	41.1	30	46.2
Total chains	107	100.0	65	100.0

Table 2: Result of manual analysis of incongruences.

around 80% of the extracted incongruences, and implicitation around 20%. However, the extracted incongruences might contain phenomena not related to the annotation or the translations itself. In the following section we present a manual analysis to investigate this further.

5.2 Manual analysis

We select a set of overlapping and unpaired chains from a TED text and from several news texts[4] for our manual analysis. The cases are classified according to the four categories defined in Section 2 above. We summarise their distributions in Table 2. We also try to identify the reasons for the specific incongruences.

Explicitation The results of the manual analysis, however, show that 37.4% of the analysed TED talk chains and 41.5% chains in news are cases of explicitation – German translations are longer than the corresponding English sources, and thus, they contain additional elements of coreference chains. Most of these cases are represented by relative clauses as illustrated in example (2) in Section 2 above. In this example, we find a nonfinite construction in English that has to be transferred into German and has no equivalent construction. Non-finite constructions contain participles and also infinitives like the one in example (8). These are cases of obligatory explicitation.

(8) a. *[the first one in his family] to go to college.*
b. *[der Erste in seiner Familie], [der] an einer Universität studierte.*

Our data also contains examples where a relative pronoun is omitted in English, as in example (9). The mismatch between the chains is not caused by the difference of the constructions used – there are relative clauses in both the source and the target. The difference is in the degree of explicitation of this clause – English does not require a relative pronoun, whereas German does. Therefore, a translator has to make the German target sentence more explicit.

(9) a. *Those are [things] you have in common with your parents and with your children.*
b. *[Dinge], [die] Sie mit Ihren Eltern und Kindern gemein haben.*

Example (10) illustrates another mismatch between relative clauses in English and German. In this case, the relative clause is not obligatory, and we describe it as a case of non-obligatory explicitation: There is a temporal clause introduced with *those moments... when* in the source, which is transferred with a relative clause (with a locative function) into German: *jene Momente... in denen.* The temporal clause does not belong to a coreference chain and is, therefore, not annotated in our corpus.

(10) a. *...like [those moments] in grand opera [when] the hero realizes he loves the heroine.*

[4]News texts are shorter than TED talks.

b. *...an [jene Momente] in der Oper erinnert, in [denen] der Held erkennt, dass er die Heldin liebt.*

Explicitation through relative pronouns makes up 70% of the observed cases. Further examples of explicitation include adding possessives, like in example (4) in Section 2, where the pronoun *them* is transferred into *ihre Kinder.* This is a case of non-obligatory explicitation. Example (11) contains a similar transformation pattern (*parenting – ihre Mutterrolle*) with a different source of explicitation. In English, *parenting my brother and me* does not require any modifier, whereas the German noun phrase *Mutterrolle für ich und meinen Bruder* requires either the definite article *the* or the possessive pronoun *ihre.* In this way, German is more explicit.

(11) a. *...[my mother] used to say... I took it as the greatest compliment in the world that [she] would say that about parenting my brother and me.*

b. *sagte [meine Mutter] immer... Als Kind nahm ich das als das größte Kompliment, dass [sie] so [ihre] Mutterrolle für mich und meinen Bruder beschreiben würde.*

Implicitation Implicitation comprises 6.5% in the analysed TED talks and 12.3% in the analysed news. In most cases, we observe omission of the subject pronoun in the German sentence, and a verb phrase is used instead of a clause, see example (12). In the English sentence, the first relative clause introduced with *who* contains a verb in passive voice, whereas the second has an active verb. Therefore, the second subject expressed through the relative pronoun *who* is necessary here. In the German translations, both clauses are active.

(12) a. *[mice] [who] have been given that substance and [who] have the achondroplasia gene, grow to full size.*

b. *[Mäuse], [die] diesen Wirkstoff erhalten haben, und das Achondroplasie-Gen aufweisen.*

In example (13), both English and German sentences contain clauses that have the same verb tense and voice. However, the translator decided to omit the subject in the target.

(13) a. *And [Sue] looked at the floor, and [she] thought for a minute.*

b. *Und [Sue] schaute auf den Boden und dachte eine Minute nach.*

Simplifying syntax by merging sentences is recommended as a strategy for subtitle compression[5]. Thus, the analysed cases of implicitation in our data could be genre-specific.

Different interpretations Differences in how the source and the target text were interpreted only affect the incongruences in the analysed TED talk (15%) and do not occur in the news sample. These are mostly cases of overlapping chains containing more German mentions or German unpaired chains. In example (14), the annotator identified different antecedents in the source and the target sentence. The English chain contains two elements – a split antecedent that consists of three noun phrases (*self-acceptance, family acceptance* and *social acceptance*) and the anaphor *they* referring to them. The German chain starts in the previous sentence and has the antecedent *drei Stufen der Akzeptanz* that corresponds to *three levels of acceptance* which is not marked in the English sentence, the anaphor *die* that corresponds to the English relative *that* and the anaphor *die drei* corresponding to the pronoun *they* in the English source. Both chain variants can be considered as correct chains depending on how the text is interpreted.

(14) a. *...that there were three levels of acceptance that needed to take place. There's [self-acceptance]$_1$, there's [family acceptance]$_1$, and there's [social acceptance]$_1$. And [they]$_1$ don't always coincide.*

b. *dass es [drei Stufen der Akzeptanz]$_2$ gibt, [die]$_2$ alle zum Tragen kommen mussten. Da war die Eigenakzeptanz, die Akzeptanz der Familie und die gesellschaftliche Akzeptanz. Und [die drei]$_2$ überschneiden sich nicht immer.*

The scope of a relation can be interpreted in a different way, if an anaphor is ambiguous. In example (15), the pronoun *it* refers to an event which might be expressed by either *putting ... away* or *is put away.* The annotator marks the first one in the

[5]See `https://translations.ted.com/How_to_Compress_Subtitles#Simplifying_the_syntax`

English source and the second in the German target. The latter is expressed via the deverbal noun *Weggeben* ("putting away"), which is annotated as a nominal antecedent.

(15) a. *"There is no reason to feel guilty about [putting a Down syndrome child away]$_1$ whether it is put away in the sense of hidden in a sanitarium... [It]$_1$ is sad, yes – dreadful. But [it]$_1$ carries no guilt.*

b. *"Es gibt keinen Grund, sich schuldig zu fühlen, wenn man ein Kind mit Down-Syndrom weggibt, egal ob es sich dabei um [ein " Weggeben"]$_2$ im Sinne von 'in einem Heim verstecken" handelt... [Es]$_2$ ist traurig, ja – und schrecklich. Aber [es]$_2$ entbehrt jeder Schuld.*

Annotation error The analysed incongruences contain 43% of annotation errors (44% in the TED talk and 30% in the news). These errors can be classified into the following categories: (a) different chain membership as illustrated in example (7) in Section 2 above; (b) non-marked mentions or chains – annotation is missing in either English or German; and (c) incorrectly marked mentions. The first case is especially frequent in overlapping chains (containing both more English and German mentions). The second error type is represented mostly by the unpaired German chains. The last error category is scattered across different types of incongruences.

6 Conclusion and Discussion

In this paper, we analysed incongruences in parallel coreference annotation and suggested a typology based on their sources. The results showed that many incongruences in our data are due to explicitation, i.e., German translations contain more explicit linguistic means that trigger coreference. We also showed that explicitation has its origin either in language typology – idiosyncracies between the two languages under analysis in terms of coreference, or in the translation process. Besides that, we detected differences in the interpretation of the source and target texts along with annotation errors. They both result from the way the annotation was performed – although the annotation scheme includes universal categories for both languages, the annotation process itself was not parallel, and the source and the target texts were annotated independently. This raises the question of annotation strategies, when working cross-lingually. Could those incongruences be avoided if the work were performed in parallel? This would require the annotators to have a very good command of both languages. However, parallel annotation could cause different problems, e.g., by biasing the annotation of the target text excessively towards the source. Another option is to annotate texts independently and then cross-check them in parallel, which might help to detect chains and mentions that were "overseen" in the independent annotation procedure.

In the future, we aim at automating the classification of the extracted incongruences according to the suggested typology. Automatic extraction of annotation error candidates can also help in the improvement of the existing annotation and saves time, as the annotators do not have to read all the texts from scratch, which reduces manual correction effort.

Moreover, we plan to analyse more texts manually to find out if the incongruence categories are systemic across the whole corpus at hand. As there is a subcorpus of news in our data, we can also investigate genre-related effects. Furthermore, we will perform analysis of further types of coreference chains, i.e. non-entity coreference. Although annotated in our data, they were excluded from analysis for practical reasons.

Another extension of the study includes analysis of the differences in the type of referring expressions in parallel chains, as mentioned in Section 5.1 above. Non-equivalence of the referring expressions in parallel chains represents coreference transformations in English-German translations (for instance, a nominal phrase in English is translated as a pronoun in German, etc.). This kind of information is valuable for contrastive linguistics and translation studies as it delivers information on different strategies in information status presentation in English and German.

The problem of making annotations of parallel texts consistent across languages was here studied in the context of coreference annotation, but it clearly poses a challenge for all types of multilingual linguistic annotation. More systematic and automatic methods to improve cross-lingual annotation congruence have the potential to benefit applications and research in language technology, contrastive linguistics and translation studies alike.

References

Marco Baroni and Silvia Bernardini. 2006. A new approach to the study of translationese: Machine-learning the difference between original and translated text. *Literary and Linguistic Computing*, 21(3):259–274.

Shoshana Blum-Kulka. 1986. Shifts of cohesion and coherence in translation. In J. House and S. Blum-Kulka, editors, *Interlingual and intercultural communication*, pages 17–35. Gunter Narr, Tübingen.

Stefanie Dipper and Heike Zinsmeister. 2012. Annotating abstract anaphora. *Language Resources and Evaluation*, 46(1):37–52.

Martin Durrell. 2011. *Hammer's German Grammar and Usage*, 5 edition. Routledge, London and New York.

Yulia Grishina and Manfred Stede. 2015. Knowledge-lean projection of coreference chains across languages. In *Proceedings of the 8th Workshop on Building and Using Comparable Corpora*, page 14, Beijing, China.

Yulia Grishina and Manfred Stede. 2017. Multi-source annotation projection of coreference chains: assessing strategies and testing opportunities. In *Proceedings of the 2nd Workshop on Coreference Resolution Beyond OntoNotes (CORBON 2017)*, pages 41–50. Association for Computational Linguistics.

Iustina Ilisei, Diana Inkpen, Gloria Corpas Pastor, and Ruslan Mitkov. 2010. Identification of translationese: A machine learning approach. In *Computational linguistics and intelligent text processing*, pages 503–511. Springer Berlin Heidelberg.

Kinga Klaudy. 2008. Explicitation. In M. Baker and G. Saldanha, editors, *Routledge Encyclopedia of Translation Studies*, 2 edition, pages 104–108. Routledge, London & New York.

Kinga Klaudy and Krisztina Károly. 2005. Implicitation in translation: Empirical evidence for operational asymmetry in translation. *Across Languages and Cultures*, 6:13–28.

Philipp Koehn. 2010. *Machine Translation*. Cambridge University Press, Cambridge.

Philipp Koehn, Amittai Axelrod, Alexandra Birch Mayne, Chris Callison-Burch, Miles Osborne, and David Talbot. 2005. Edinburgh system description for the 2005 IWSLT speech translation evaluation. In *International Workshop on Spoken Language Translation*, Pittsburgh, Pennsylvania.

Kerstin Kunz. 2010. *Variation in English and German Nominal Coreference: A Study of Political Essays*. Saarbrücker Beiträge zur Sprach- und Translationswissenschaft. Peter Lang.

Kerstin Kunz and Ekaterina Lapshinova-Koltunski. 2015. Cross-linguistic analysis of discourse variation across registers. *Special Issue of Nordic Journal of English Studies*, 14(1):258–288.

Kerstin Kunz and Erich Steiner. 2012. Towards a comparison of cohesive reference in English and German: System and text. In M. Taboada, S. Doval Suárez, and E. González Álvarez, editors, *Contrastive Discourse Analysis. Functional and Corpus Perspectives*. Equinox, London.

Ekaterina Lapshinova-Koltunski and Christian Hardmeier. 2017. *Coreference Corpus Annotation Guidelines*.

Ekaterina Lapshinova-Koltunski, Christian Hardmeier, and Pauline Krielke. 2018. ParCorFull: a parallel corpus annotated with full coreference. In *Proceedings of 11th Language Resources and Evaluation Conference*, pages 423–428, Miyazaki, Japan. European Language Resources Association (ELRA).

Michael Novák and Anna Nedoluzhko. 2015. Correspondences between Czech and English coreferential expressions. *Discours*, 16.

Michal Novák. 2018. A fine-grained large-scale analysis of coreference projection. In *Proceedings of the First Workshop on Computational Models of Reference, Anaphora and Coreference*, pages 77–86, New Orleans, Louisiana. Association for Computational Linguistics.

Franz Josef Och and Hermann Ney. 2003. A systematic comparison of various statistical alignment models. *Computational Linguistics*, 29:19–51.

Maciej Ogrodniczuk. 2013. Translation- and projection-based unsupervised coreference resolution for Polish. *Language Processing and Intelligent Information Systems, IIS 2013*, 7912.

Oana Postolache, Dan Cristea, and Constantin Orasan. 2006. Tranferring coreference chains through word alignment. In *Proceedings of the 5th International Conference on Language Resources and Evaluation*.

David Yarowsky, Grace Ngai, and Richard Wicentowski. 2001. Inducing multilingual text analysis tools via robust projection across aligned corpora. In *Proceedings of the First International Conference on Human Language Technology Research*.

Šárka Zikánová, Eva Hajičová, Barbora Hladká, Pavlína Jínová, Jiří Mírovský, Anna Nedoluzhko, Lucie Poláková, Kateřina Rysová, Magdaléna Rysová, and Jan Václ. 2015. *Discourse and Coherence. From the Sentence Structure to Relations in Text*. ÚFAL, Praha, Czechia.

Deep Cross-Lingual Coreference Resolution for Less-Resourced Languages: The Case of Basque

Gorka Urbizu, Ander Soraluze and Olatz Arregi
Ixa group, University of the Basque Country (UPV/EHU)
gurbizu002@ikasle.ehu.eus
{ander.soraluze, olatz.arregi}@ehu.eus

Abstract

In this paper, we present a cross-lingual neural coreference resolution system for a less-resourced language such as Basque. To begin with, we build the first neural coreference resolution system for Basque, training it with the relatively small EPEC-KORREF corpus (45,000 words). Next, a cross-lingual coreference resolution system is designed. With this approach, the system learns from a bigger English corpus, using cross-lingual embeddings, to perform the coreference resolution for Basque. The cross-lingual system obtains slightly better results (40.93 F1 CoNLL) than the monolingual system (39.12 F1 CoNLL), without using any Basque language corpus to train it.

1 Introduction

Coreference resolution, the task of identifying and clustering all the expressions referring to the same real-world entity in a text, is essential in any Natural Language Processing (NLP) task that includes language understanding. For instance, tasks such as text summarisation (Steinberger et al., 2007), question answering (Vicedo and Ferrández, 2006), sentiment analysis (Nicolov et al., 2008) or machine translation (Werlen and Popescu-Belis, 2017) can benefit from coreference resolution.

In the last few years, we have witnessed how the revolution of neural networks and deep learning has improved the previous results in almost any NLP task. Big improvements in results were also obtained in coreference resolution in the last two years using neural approaches, mainly for English.

Although there is work in progress in languages other than English using neural networks, the results obtained are not so good in all of them. This is mostly due to smaller corpus sizes, which affects neural approaches negatively. The situation of less-resourced languages is even harder, as they have smaller datasets and annotating them is an arduous task to carry out by hand.

In this paper, we present a monolingual neural coreference resolution system for Basque. Subsequently, we try a cross-lingual approach to analyze whether it is possible to build a language independent coreference resolution system that obtains competent results when applied to less-resourced languages. To this end, we build a system which learns exclusively from an English corpus and apply it to resolve coreference in Basque texts. Afterwards, we compare the results of the monolingual system with a small dataset of the target language, and those of the cross-lingual system that learns from a bigger available corpus of another language, but not the target language.

The paper is organized as follows. Section 2 introduces related work. Section 3 describes the model built for coreference resolution. In section 4, we present the monolingual and cross-lingual experimental setups. Section 5 contains the obtained results. Finally, Section 6 presents our conclusions and future work.

2 Related Work

Coreference resolution has been handled with different techniques during the last few decades until deep learning techniques spread in the field. Among the most influential works are the rule-based system by H. Lee et al. (2013) and machine learning based systems by Soon et al. (2001) and Versley et al. (2008).

One of the first successful neural coreference resolution system (Wiseman et al.) obtained state-of-the-art results. Similar works followed, and although they differ in the method used for generating instances, all of them worked with automatic mentions and rule-based extracted features as input to a feedforward deep neural architecture (Clark and Manning; Wiseman et al., 2016).

The coreference resolution system that obtains

Proceedings of the 2nd Workshop on Computational Models of Reference, Anaphora and Coreference (CRAC 2019), pages 35–41, Minneapolis, USA, June 7, 2019.

the best results in the current state-of-the-art is an end-to-end neural system, which is presented in K. Lee et al. (2017) and K. Lee et al. (2018). This system does not use any automatically preprocessed mentions or features, and it is able to find the needed features in the raw text, so it does not need any annotation other than the coreferential relations in the corpus. This manner, error propagation from the features extraction is reduced by learning those within the same neural network.

Neural coreference resolution systems for other languages have been created as well. For instance, in Clark and Manning they develop a system for Chinese, in Park et al. (2016) for Korean, and in Nitoń et al. (2018) for Polish.

Moreover, there has been some recent research to build cross-lingual systems for coreference resolution, as cross-lingual transfer learning has given good results in some other NLP tasks such as machine translation or language modeling (Lample and Conneau, 2019). Cruz et al. (2018) used neural networks to solve coreference for Portuguese by learning from Spanish, a related language, using cross-lingual word embeddings. Kundu et al. presented a similar system for Spanish and Chinese using English for training.

As regards the Basque language, this is the first work about neural coreference resolution. Nevertheless, a rule-based coreference resolution system (Soraluze et al., 2015) and a machine learning based system (Soraluze et al., 2016) have been developed. Both of which used a rule-based mention detector (Soraluze et al., 2017).

3 Model

In this section, the neural coreference resolution model, which is used for the experiments carried out, is presented.

The model used for coreference resolution for Basque is based on the neural system developed for Polish (Nitoń et al., 2018). After considering and discarting different models, it was chosen because both languages share some features such as being agglutinative or having free word order, and it obtained competitive results.

We use the mention-pair model to create instances, as in (Nitoń et al., 2018). They demonstrated that the mention-pair model obtains better results than the entity-mention for Polish.

In our case, gold mentions are used for training and development sets, and gold and automatic mentions are used for the test set, so we can see the effect of the performance of the mention detector in the results.

Once mention pairs are created, we extract some features of each mention and the mention pair to feed the neural network. In this work, we use pretrained 300-dimensional FastText embeddings (Bojanowski et al., 2017). They work with substring information, and this gives better results with morphologically rich languages such as Basque.

For each mention, we extract the following features:

- An average of the embeddings of the words that make up the mention (300 dimensions).
- An average of the embeddings of the words in the sentence in which the mention appears (300).

We extract the following features for the mention pair:

- Distance in words between the mentions, represented as binary features[1] (11).
- Distance in mentions between the mentions, represented as binary features (11).
- Whether mentions are in the same sentence (1).
- String matching (1).
- Lemma matching (1).
- Language[2]: Basque or English (1).

These features are easy to obtain for any language, and need very little preprocessing, just the lemmatization. In total, we obtain instances of 1,226 dimensions.

3.1 Neural Network

In this work, we use a fully connected network of 3 hidden layers, with 500, 300 and 100 neurons in each, and a single neuron in the output layer. The neural network takes instances of 1,226 dimensions in the input layer, and it returns a number between 0 and 1 in the output. The activation functions used are ReLU in the hidden layers and

[1]Binned into one of the following slots [0,1,2,3,4,5-7,8-15,16-31,32-63,64+,discontinuous].

[2]Included with the purpose of training on mixed language corpus in the future.

sigmoid in the output layer. ReLU function computes a positive number, while sigmoid function computes a number between 0 and 1.

$$\text{Input vector: } x = [e_i, e_j, e_{ij}]$$

$$\text{1st hidden layer: } h_1 = \mathrm{ReLU}(W_1^T x + b_1)$$

$$\text{2nd hidden layer: } h_2 = \mathrm{ReLU}(W_2^T h_1 + b_2)$$

$$\text{3rd hidden layer: } h_3 = \mathrm{ReLU}(W_3^T h_2 + b_3)$$

$$\text{Output layer: } p(i,j) = sigmoid(w^T h_3)$$

Where e_i and e_j are the features of each mention, e_{ij} the features of the mention pair, W the weights and b the biases.

The neural network was trained to minimize the binary cross-entropy function. We trained the model for 2 epochs using a mini-batch size of 64. We used Adam optimization (Kingma and Ba, 2014), batch-normalization (Ioffe and Szegedy, 2015), and a dropout rate (Srivastava et al., 2014) of 0.2. The neural network was implemented using python library *KERAS*[3].

The mention pairs with a higher value than a threshold in the predictions are grouped in the same coreference cluster in testing time. To obtain the optimal threshold values, we used the development set.

4 Experimental Setup

Two experiments were carried out, both in similar conditions to be able to compare the outputs. In the first experiment, we trained the model described in the previous section with the available corpus of the Basque language for coreference. After that, we trained the system using a big corpus of English to see if the coreference resolution task could be learnt using transfer learning from another language.

4.1 Corpora

For the next experiments two corpora for coreference resolution are used, the EPEC-KORREF corpus (Ceberio et al., 2018) for Basque, the target language, and the OntoNotes English corpus (Hovy et al., 2006).

EPEC-KORREF[4] corpus is a Basque corpus, composed of news, of around 45K words and 12K mentions, which has mentions and coreferential relations, including singletons, annotated. The corpus is already divided into training, development and test sets, more details about the partition are shown in Table 1.

	Words	Mentions	Clusters	Singletons
Train	23,520	6,525	1,011	3,401
Dev	6,914	1,907	302	982
Test	15,949	4,360	621	2,445
Total	46,383	12,792	1,934	6,828

Table 1: EPEC-KORREF corpus

OntoNotes corpus is an English corpus with text from a variety of domains of more than one million words, with annotated mentions and coreferential relations. We used only newswire (nw), and broadcast news (bn) sets, avoiding conversation sets, in order to have texts of the same domain (around 825K words and 100K mentions). The details about the corpus are shown in Table 2.

	Words	Mentions
nw	625,000	75,000
bn	200,000	24,000

Table 2: OntoNotes corpus

4.2 Monolingual System

To develop the monolingual system, the neural model presented in Section 3 was trained on the EPEC-KORREF Basque corpus. In Figure 1, we can see how a train instance is generated from a coreferential mention pair of the following sentence:

Gaur egungo 15 herrialdeetatik 27ra igaro beharko du erdiko epera [Europar Batasunak], Europa ekialdeko eta hego ekialdeko 12 herrialde [bere] baitan hartuta.

"From the 15 countries of today, the [European Union] will have to change to 27 in the medium term, taking on [its] own 12 countries from west and southwest Europe."

The threshold for clustering mentions referring to the same entity was settled at 0.5 in the development set.

4.3 Cross-Lingual System

The same neural model presented in Section 3 is used to develop the cross-lingual system. However, in this case, it is trained on the English corpus, without using any corpus of the target lan-

[3]https://keras.io/

[4]http://ixa.si.ehu.es/node/4487

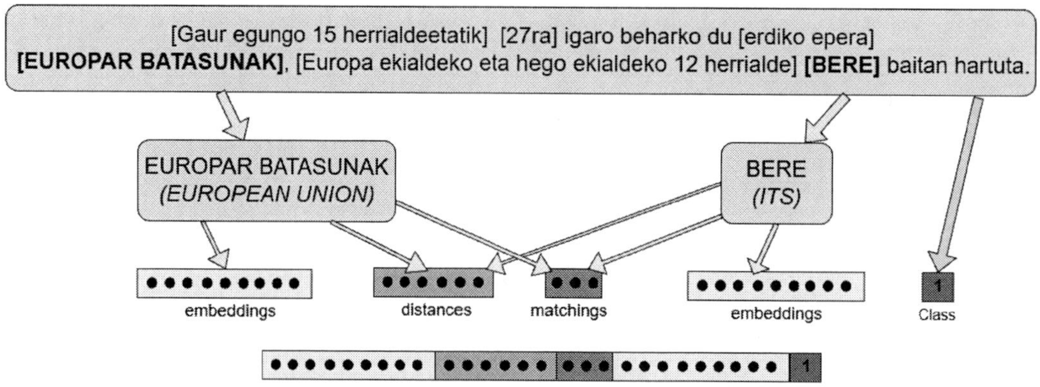

Figure 1: Example of an instance for a positive mention pair

guage, for the task of coreference resolution for Basque.

For this purpose, we use cross-lingual embeddings, as the language in the training set and the test set is different. We did this using the VecMap tool (Artetxe et al., 2018), which maps embeddings of one language to the other without using any bilingual dictionary.

The threshold for clustering coreferential mentions was settled at 0.9 in the development set.

5 Results

The coreference clusters obtained in the output of each experiment were evaluated with the official scorer proposed by Pradhan et al. (2014) for coreference resolution, and we also added the more recent LEA metric.

The main metrics used in the task are MUC (Vilain et al., 1995), B^3 (Bagga and Baldwin, 1998), $CEAF_m$ and $CEAF_e$ (Luo, 2005), BLANC (Recasens and Hovy, 2011), LEA (Moosavi and Strube) and CoNLL, which is the average of MUC, B^3 and $CEAF_e$ (Denis and Baldridge, 2009).

The results for the monolingual system and the cross-lingual system are shown in Table 4.

Our monolingual system obtains 39.12 F1 and 53.19 F1 for the CoNLL metric with automatic mentions and gold mentions respectively. The difference of using automatic (F1 = 73.79) or gold mentions is considerable (more than 14 points), which shows the importance of mention detection in the results. Furthermore, the low values for MUC metric stand out, which shows that the model does create a small number of coreference links.

Similar results were obtained for the cross-lingual system. The results for some metrics, such as MUC, decrease slightly, while the results for other metrics, such as LEA, increase a bit. Our cross-lingual system obtains 40.93 F1 for the CoNLL metric when automatic mentions are used and 54.46 F1 with gold mentions. We obtain better results with the cross-lingual system without using the target language corpus for the training than when using the small corpus available for Basque.

Moreover, to contextualize the results we obtained, in Table 3, we can see the results of the neural cross-lingual system in comparison with previous coreference resolution systems for Basque. The results obtained are lower than those obtained by previous rule-based (Soraluze et al., 2015) and ML-based (Soraluze et al., 2016) systems with the same corpus.

System	**CoNLL** (auto)	(gold)
Rule-based	55.98	76.51
ML-based	54.21	73.94
Neural cross-lingual	40.93	54.46

Table 3: Comparison with previous systems for Basque

In Table 5 we can see an example of the type of mistakes in the output of our cross-lingual system. Key refers to gold annotation and response to the output of the system. Parentheses are used to mark mentions and numbers to tag coreference clusters. In the given example, we can see that the system has problems to link pronouns to the coreference cluster that they belong. This mistakes at solving pronominal coreference, are more common with neural and ML approaches than in rule-based sys-

System	MD	MUC	B^3	$CEAF_m$	$CEAF_e$	BLANC	LEA	CoNLL
Monolingual (auto)	73.79	9.72	54.83	49.66	52.81	29.41	29.40	39.12
Cross-lingual (auto)		8.30	58.61	53.27	55.87	29.14	36.34	40.93
Monolingual (gold)	100	15.81	74.60	63.10	69.17	53.28	39.87	53.19
Cross-lingual (gold)		10.00	79.90	68.09	73.47	51.91	49.30	54.46

Table 4: Results of monolingual and cross-lingual systems for gold and automatic mentions

Key	... eta (bera $)_1$, ((zailtasun hori $)_2$ gainditu duen munduko lehen emakumea $)_1$.
Response	... eta (bera $)_1$, (zailtasun hori $)_2$ gainditu duen (munduko lehen emakumea $)_3$.
Translation	... and (she $)_1$ is (the first woman in the world to overcome (that difficulty $)_2$ $)_1$.

Table 5: Example of mistakes in the output

tems. Training our cross-lingual system on English might make this even harder, as Basque has gender-neutral pronouns and it is quite common to drop pronouns at subject or object positions.

6 Conclusions and Future Work

We present a neural coreference resolution system for Basque, and a cross-lingual system, which is trained on a bigger English corpus.

The results obtained with both systems are significantly lower than those obtained by previous non-neural systems for Basque. The results of the cross-lingual system (40.93 F1 CoNLL) are slightly better than the monolingual ones (39.12 F1 CoNLL), and this was obtained without using any target language corpus in the training phase.

Furthermore, we conclude that the corpus for Basque, of 45,000 words, is too small for a monolingual neural approach. Thus, the results obtained with the cross-lingual system are outstanding, as they improved the results obtained without using any corpus of the target language.

An in-depth error analysis needs to be done to understand better the results of both systems. Moreover, training the same model for coreference resolution for English would help to see whether the results obtained were due to the neural architecture and the model, or the small corpus and the cross-lingual approach. In addition, it might be interesting to see what results we would obtain with a simpler model, mostly for the monolingual system.

The cross-lingual approach needs to be investigated further. We are planning to apply this cross-lingual approach to the state-of-the-art neural network architecture (K. Lee et al., 2018), which might learn better, and could help to close the gap between results obtained with automatic and gold mentions.

Finally, this cross-lingual system could be tested for different language pairs, to see what language pairs give better results, with the aim of building a universal coreference resolution system, which would learn the task for many languages and resolve coreference for any other language.

Acknowledgments

This research was partially supported by the Spanish Ministry of Economy and Competitiveness (MINECO/FEDER, UE; PROSA-MED project, TIN2016-77820-C3-1-R) and by the European Commission (LINGUATEC project, EFA227/16).

We thank the three anonymous reviewers whose comments and suggestions contributed to improve this work.

References

Mikel Artetxe, Gorka Labaka, and Eneko Agirre. 2018. A robust self-learning method for fully unsupervised cross-lingual mappings of word embeddings. In *Proceedings of the 56th Annual Meeting of the Association for Computational Linguistics (Volume 1: Long Papers)*, pages 789–798.

Amit Bagga and Breck Baldwin. 1998. Entity-based cross-document coreferencing using the vector space model. In *Proceedings of the 36th Annual Meeting of the Association for Computational Linguistics and 17th International Conference on Computational Linguistics-Volume 1*, pages 79–85. Association for Computational Linguistics.

Piotr Bojanowski, Edouard Grave, Armand Joulin, and Tomas Mikolov. 2017. Enriching word vectors with subword information. *Transactions of the Association for Computational Linguistics*, 5:135–146.

Klara Ceberio, Itziar Aduriz, Arantza Díaz de Ilarraza, and Ines Garcia-Azkoaga. 2018. Coreferential relations in Basque: the annotation process. *Journal of psycholinguistic research*, 47(2):325–342.

Kevin Clark and Christopher D Manning. Improving Coreference Resolution by Learning Entity-Level Distributed Representations. In *Proceedings of the 54th Annual Meeting of the Association for Computational Linguistics (Volume 1: Long Papers)*.

André Ferreira Cruz, Gil Rocha, and Henrique Lopes Cardoso. 2018. Exploring Spanish corpora for Portuguese coreference resolution. In *2018 Fifth International Conference on Social Networks Analysis, Management and Security (SNAMS)*, pages 290–295. IEEE.

Pascal Denis and Jason Baldridge. 2009. Global joint models for coreference resolution and named entity classification. *Procesamiento del Lenguaje Natural*, 42:87–96.

Eduard Hovy, Mitchell Marcus, Martha Palmer, Lance Ramshaw, and Ralph Weischedel. 2006. Ontonotes: The 90% solution. In *Proceedings of the Human Language Technology Conference of the NAACL, Companion Volume: Short Papers*.

Sergey Ioffe and Christian Szegedy. 2015. Batch Normalization: Accelerating Deep Network Training by Reducing Internal Covariate Shift. In *Proceedings of the 32nd International Conference on Machine Learning, ICML 2015, Lille, France, 6-11 July 2015*, pages 448–456.

Diederik Kingma and Jimmy Ba. 2014. Adam: A method for stochastic optimization. *International Conference on Learning Representations*.

Gourab Kundu, Avi Sil, Radu Florian, and Wael Hamza. Neural cross-lingual coreference resolution and its application to entity linking. In *Proceedings of the 56th Annual Meeting of the Association for Computational Linguistics (Volume 2: Short Papers)*.

Guillaume Lample and Alexis Conneau. 2019. Cross-lingual language model pretraining. *arXiv preprint arXiv:1901.07291*.

Heeyoung Lee, Angel Chang, Yves Peirsman, Nathanael Chambers, Mihai Surdeanu, and Dan Jurafsky. 2013. Deterministic coreference resolution based on entity-centric, precision-ranked rules. *Computational Linguistics*, 39(4):885–916.

Kenton Lee, Luheng He, Mike Lewis, and Luke Zettlemoyer. 2017. End-to-end Neural Coreference Resolution. In *Proceedings of the 2017 Conference on Empirical Methods in Natural Language Processing*, pages 188–197.

Kenton Lee, Luheng He, and Luke Zettlemoyer. 2018. Higher-order coreference resolution with coarse-to-fine inference. In *NAACL-HLT (2)*, pages 687–692. Association for Computational Linguistics.

Xiaoqiang Luo. 2005. On coreference resolution performance metrics. In *Proceedings of the Conference on Human Language Technology and Empirical Methods in Natural Language Processing*, pages 25–32. Association for Computational Linguistics.

Nafise Sadat Moosavi and Michael Strube. Which coreference evaluation metric do you trust? a proposal for a link-based entity aware metric. In *Proceedings of the 54th Annual Meeting of the Association for Computational Linguistics (Volume 1: Long Papers)*.

Nicolas Nicolov, Franco Salvetti, and Steliana Ivanova. 2008. Sentiment Analysis: Does Coreference Matter? In *AISB 2008 Convention Communication, Interaction and Social Intelligence*, pages 37–40.

Bartłomiej Nitoń, Paweł Morawiecki, and Maciej Ogrodniczuk. 2018. Deep neural networks for coreference resolution for Polish. In *Proceedings of the Eleventh International Conference on Language Resources and Evaluation (LREC-2018)*, pages 395–400.

Cheoneum Park, KyoungHo Choi, Changki Lee, and Soojong Lim. 2016. Korean Coreference Resolution with Guided Mention Pair Model Using Deep Learning. *ETRI Journal*, 38(6):1207–1217.

Sameer Pradhan, Xiaoqiang Luo, Marta Recasens, Eduard Hovy, Vincent Ng, and Michael Strube. 2014. Scoring Coreference Partitions of Predicted Mentions: A Reference Implementation. In *Proceedings of the 52nd Annual Meeting of the Association for Computational Linguistics (Volume 2: Short Papers)*, pages 30–35, Baltimore, Maryland. Association for Computational Linguistics.

Marta Recasens and Eduard Hovy. 2011. BLANC: Implementing the Rand index for coreference evaluation. *Natural Language Engineering*, 17(4):485–510.

Wee Meng Soon, Hwee Tou Ng, and Daniel Chung Yong Lim. 2001. A machine learning approach to coreference resolution of noun phrases. *Computational linguistics*, 27(4):521–544.

Ander Soraluze, Olatz Arregi, Xabier Arregi, and Arantza Diaz de Ilarraza. 2015. Coreference Resolution for Morphologically Rich Languages. Adaptation of the Stanford System to Basque. In *Procesamiento del Lenguaje Natural*, volume 55, pages 23–30.

Ander Soraluze, Olatz Arregi, Xabier Arregi, and Arantza Díaz de Ilarraza. 2017. Improving mention detection for Basque based on a deep error analysis. *Natural Language Engineering*, 23(3):351–384.

Ander Soraluze, Olatz Arregi, Xabier Arregi, Arantza Diaz de Ilarraza, Mijail Kabadjov, and Massimo Poesio. 2016. Coreference Resolution for the Basque Language with BART. In *Proceedings of the Workshop on Coreference Resolution Beyond OntoNotes (CORBON 2016)*, pages 67–73.

Nitish Srivastava, Geoffrey Hinton, Alex Krizhevsky, Ilya Sutskever, and Ruslan Salakhutdinov. 2014. Dropout: a simple way to prevent neural networks from overfitting. *The Journal of Machine Learning Research*, 15(1):1929–1958.

Josef Steinberger, Massimo Poesio, Mijail A. Kabadjov, and Karel Jeek. 2007. Two Uses of Anaphora Resolution in Summarization. *Information Processing and Management*, 43(6):1663–1680.

Yannick Versley, Simone Paolo Ponzetto, Massimo Poesio, Vladimir Eidelman, Alan Jern, Jason Smith, Xiaofeng Yang, and Alessandro Moschitti. 2008. BART: A modular toolkit for coreference resolution. In *Proceedings of the 46th Annual Meeting of the Association for Computational Linguistics on Human Language Technologies: Demo Session*, pages 9–12. Association for Computational Linguistics.

Jose Vicedo and Antonio Ferrández. 2006. Coreference In Q&A. In *Advances in Open Domain Question Answering*, volume 32 of *Text, Speech and Language Technology*, pages 71–96. Springer.

Marc Vilain, John Burger, John Aberdeen, Dennis Connolly, and Lynette Hirschman. 1995. A model-theoretic coreference scoring scheme. In *Proceedings of the 6th Conference on Message Understanding*, pages 45–52. Association for Computational Linguistics.

Lesly Miculicich Werlen and Andrei Popescu-Belis. 2017. Using coreference links to improve Spanish-to-English machine translation. In *Proceedings of the 2nd Workshop on Coreference Resolution Beyond OntoNotes (CORBON 2017)*, pages 30–40.

Sam Wiseman, Alexander M Rush, Stuart Shieber, and Jason Weston. Learning Anaphoricity and Antecedent Ranking Features for Coreference Resolution. In *Proceedings of the 53rd Annual Meeting of the Association for Computational Linguistics and the 7th International Joint Conference on Natural Language Processing (Volume 1: Long Papers)*.

Sam Wiseman, Alexander M Rush, and Stuart M Shieber. 2016. Learning Global Features for Coreference Resolution. In *Proceedings of the 2016 Conference of the North American Chapter of the Association for Computational Linguistics: Human Language Technologies*, pages 994–1004.

Author Index

Association for Computational Linguistics
209 N. Eighth Street
Stroudsburg, Pennsylvania 18360

CURRAN ASSOCIATES INC. proceedings.com

ISBN 978-1-5108-8782-4

9 781510 887824